OXFORD
UNIVERSITY PRESS

English File

Beginner

Workbook WITHOUT KEY

fifth edition

Christina Latham-Koenig Clive Oxenden
Jerry Lambert with Jane Hudson

Contents

Welcome to **English File** fifth edition

Student Book

Use your Student Book in class with your teacher.

Workbook

Practise **Grammar**, **Vocabulary**, and **Pronunciation** for every lesson.

Practise the ***Practical English*** for every episode.

Oxford English Hub

Go to Oxford English Hub (englishhub.oup.com) to:

- Listen to the audio for the Pronunciation exercises.
- Use the Sound Bank videos to practise English sounds.
- Watch the Practical English videos before you do the exercises.

1A Nice to meet you

Ⓖ verb *be* (singular): *I* and *you*
Ⓥ numbers 0–10, days of the week
Ⓟ /h/, /aɪ/, and /iː/

1 GRAMMAR verb *be* (singular): *I* and *you*

a Write the sentences with contractions.

1 I am Tom.
I'm Tom.
2 You are not in class 3.
You aren't in class 3.
3 I am not Helen.
______
4 You are not a teacher.
______
5 I am Pablo.
______
6 You are in my class.
______
7 I am in room 4.
______
8 You are not Diana.
______

b Write negative [–] sentences or questions [?].

1 You're in my class. [–]
You aren't in my class.
2 You're a teacher. [?]
Are you a teacher?
3 I'm Anita. [–]
______
4 I'm in class 2. [–]
______
5 I'm in room 4. [?]
______
6 You're Dom. [?]
______
7 I'm a student. [–]
______
8 You're in class 7. [?]
______

c Complete the conversations. Use contractions where possible.

1 **A** *Are you* Andy?
B No, *I'm* Tony.

2 **A** Excuse me. ______ in number 8?
B Yes, ______. I'm Anna Jones.

3 **A** Hello, ______ Amy.
B Hi, ______ Steve. Nice to meet you.

4 **A** Hi, ______ Mia. Are you Henry?
B No, ______. I'm Max.

5 **A** Hello. ______ Lisa Gomez?
B Yes, ______. Nice to meet you.

6 **A** Hi. ______ Ben.
B Hi. ______ Rob.

7 **A** Excuse me. __________ in room 7?
B No, __________. You're in room 8.

8 **A** Excuse me. __________ my teacher?
B Yes, __________. I'm Peter Wilson.

2 VOCABULARY numbers 0–10, days of the week

a Complete the numbers with the missing vowels.

1 f _o_ _u_ r
2 t _e_ n
3 n __ n __
4 o n __
5 t h r __ __
6 t w __
7 e __ g h t
8 s __ x
9 s __ v __ n
10 z __ r __
11 f __ v __

b Write the numbers from **a** in the correct order.

0 _zero_
1 __________
2 __________
3 __________
4 __________
5 __________
6 __________
7 __________
8 __________
9 __________
10 __________

c Write the next day of the week.

1 Saturday Sunday _Monday_
2 Monday Tuesday __________
3 Thursday Friday __________
4 Sunday Monday __________
5 Friday Saturday __________
6 Tuesday Wednesday __________
7 Wednesday Thursday __________

d Answer the questions about you.

1 What's your name?
____
2 What class are you in?
____
3 What day is it today?
____
4 What days are your English classes?
____

3 PRONUNCIATION /h/, /aɪ/, and /iː/

a 🔊 **1.2** Listen and write the words in the chart.

~~five~~ **H**elen **h**ello m**ee**t n**i**ce t**ea**

1 **h**ouse	2 b**i**ke	3 tr**ee**
	five	

b 🔊 **1.3** Listen and check. Then listen again and repeat the words.

4 WORDS AND PHRASES TO LEARN

Complete the conversations with a word or phrase from the list.

Nice to meet you Sorry See you tomorrow
Thanks ~~Two cappuccinos, please~~ What's your name

1 **A** _Two cappuccinos, please_.
B OK. Just a minute.

2 **A** Hi, I'm Helen.
B Hi, I'm Rob. __________.

3 **A** Hello, I'm Sarah. __________?
B Paul.

4 **A** Goodbye. __________.
B No, Friday.
A Oh yes, sorry. See you on Friday.

5 **A** I'm not John, I'm James.
B __________.

6 **A** Tom? Your tea.
B __________.

Music round the world

G verb *be* (singular): *he*, *she*, *it*
V countries
P /ɪ/, /əʊ/, /s/, and /ʃ/

1 VOCABULARY countries

a Complete the country names.

1 M*exico*

2 E__________

3 C__________

4 S__________

5 B__________

6 J__________

7 E__________

8 N__________

b Complete the sentences with a country.

1 She's from Zurich. She's from Sw*itzerland*.
2 He's from Paris. He's from Fr__________.
3 I'm from Rome. I'm from I__________.
4 You're from Miami. You're from t__________ U__________ St__________.
5 She's from Moscow. She's from R__________.
6 He's from Istanbul. He's from T__________.
7 I'm from Warsaw. I'm from P__________.
8 You're from Cairo. You're from E__________.
9 She's from Berlin. She's from G__________.

2 GRAMMAR verb *be* (singular): *he*, *she*, *it*

a Complete the sentences with *He's*, *She's*, or *It's*.

1 *She's* from the United States.

2 *It's* from China.

3 __________ from Italy.

4 __________ from Germany.

5 __________ from Mexico.

6 __________ from Japan.

7 __________ from Spain.

8 __________ from Switzerland.

b Complete the conversations with *'s*, *is*, or *isn't*.

1 **A** Is ______ Paulo from Spain?
B No, he isn't ______. He ______ from Brazil.

2 **A** Where ______ Oaxaca? ______ it in Mexico?
B Yes, it ______.

3 **A** ______ Yasmin in the Monday class?
B No, she ______. She ______ in the Tuesday class.

4 **A** ______ your name Annie?
B No, it ______. It ______ Anna.

c Write the questions. Then answer with the information in brackets.

1 Whoopi Goldberg / from the USA? (✓ New York)
Is Whoopi Goldberg from the USA ______?
Yes, she is. She's from New York ______.

2 Kobe / in China? (✗ Japan)
Is Kobe in China ______?
No, it isn't. It's in Japan ______.

3 Salma Hayek / from Mexico? (✓ Veracruz)
______?
______.

4 Naples / in Türkiye? (✗ Italy)
______?
______.

5 Copacabana / in Brazil? (✓ Rio)
______?
______.

6 Lublin / in Nigeria? (✗ Poland)
______?
______.

7 Idris Elba / from England? (✓ London)
______?
______.

8 Geneva / in France? (✗ Switzerland)
______?
______.

9 Javier Bardem / from Spain? (✓ Las Palmas)
______?
______.

10 the Louvre / in Italy? (✗ France)
______?
______.

d Answer the questions about you.

1 Are you from England?
______

2 Where are you from (city)?
______

3 Where is it?
______

3 PRONUNCIATION /ɪ/, /əʊ/, /s/, and /ʃ/

a 1.4 Listen and circle the word with a different sound.

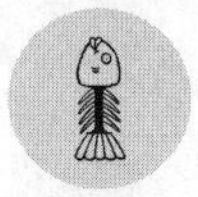 **fish**	1 Braz**i**l (Ch**i**na) **E**ngland
 ph**o**ne	2 hell**o** P**o**land tw**o**
 **s**nake	3 **s**ix Fran**c**e cla**ss**room
 **sh**ower	4 Ru**ss**ia **S**pain **sh**e

b Listen again and repeat the words.

4 WORDS AND PHRASES TO LEARN

Complete the conversations with a phrase from the list.

I don't know I think she's from Spain It's a nice city ~~Where are you from~~ Where's Basel

1 **A** Where are you from ______?
B I'm from the United States.
A Where in the United States?
B New York.
A Wow! ______.

2 **A** Is Mercedes Peón from Mexico?
B No, ______.

3 **A** Is Sapporo in China?
B Sapporo? Sorry, ______.

4 **A** ______?
B It's in Switzerland.

1 Practical English
How do you spell it?

checking into a hotel, booking a table **V** the classroom **P** the alphabet

1 PRONUNCIATION the alphabet

a 1.5 Listen and circle the letter with a different vowel sound.

	1 D E (I) V
	2 E L N X
	3 A G J K
	4 B H P D
	5 C F L S
	6 A H J Y
	7 O Q U W
	8 F T M S

b Listen again and repeat the letters.

c Say the letters in 1–5.

1 

3 

4 

2 

5 

d 1.6 Listen and check.

e 1.7 Listen and write the words in the chart.

~~hello~~ help name please she spell Spain table teacher

 1 tree	 2 egg	 3 train
	hello	

f 1.8 Listen and check. Then listen again and repeat the words.

2 VOCABULARY the classroom

a Write the words.

1 the b*oard*

2 a l________

3 a p________

4 a t________

5 the d________

6 a ch________

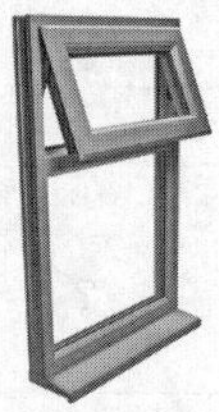

7 a w________

8 a d________y

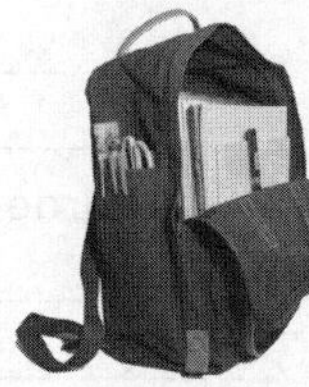

9 a b________

10 a c________

11 a p________ of p________

b **Complete the classroom expressions with the words from the list.**

books Excuse Go ~~know~~ late Look Open repeat Sit Stand spell understand

1 I don't know________.
2 Sorry? Can you ____________ that, please?
3 ____________ at the board, please.
4 ____________ your books.
5 I don't ____________.
6 How do you ____________ it?
7 ____________ to page 9.
8 Close your ____________.
9 ____________ up, please.
10 ____________ down.
11 ____________ me. What's *grazie* in English?
12 Sorry, I'm ____________.

3 CHECKING INTO A HOTEL

Complete the conversation with the words from the list.

~~evening~~ name reservation room spell surname

A Good [1]evening________.
B Hello. I have a [2]____________.
A What's your [3]____________, please?
B Wendy Mahoney.
A How do you [4]____________ your [5]____________?
B M-A-H-O-N-E-Y.
A Thank you, Ms Mahoney. You're in [6]____________ 261.
B Thanks.

4 BOOKING A TABLE

Match the questions in the conversation to answers a–e below.

A Good morning. How can I help you?
B [1] b
A What time?
B [2] ____
A OK, that's fine. What's your name, please?
B [3] ____
A OK. How many people?
B [4] ____
A Thank you, Mr Anderson. So, a table for three on Tuesday at seven?
B [5] ____

a Three.
~~b A table for Tuesday evening, please.~~
c Yes, that's great. Thanks.
d Oscar Anderson.
e Seven o'clock.

5 USEFUL PHRASES

Complete the conversations with a phrase from the list.

A table for tomorrow, please Good morning ~~How can I help you~~ How do you spell it I have a reservation Sorry Thank you That's right

1 **A** Good morning. [1]How can I help you____________?
B My name's Liam Sweeney. [2]____________ for a room for tonight.
A OK – Sweeney. [3]____________?
B S-W-E-E-N-E-Y.
A That's S-W-E-E-N-E-Y?
B [4]____________.
A OK, you're in room 49.

2 **A** [5]____________, The Green Tree restaurant. How can I help you?
B [6]____________ – for four people.
A OK. What time?
B 7.30.
A [7]____________?
B 7.30.
A [8]____________.

2A Are you on holiday?

G verb *be* (plural): *we*, *you*, *they*
V nationalities
P /dʒ/, /tʃ/, and /ʃ/

1 VOCABULARY nationalities

Complete the nationalities.

1 Maria's from Spain.
She's **S**panis____**h**.

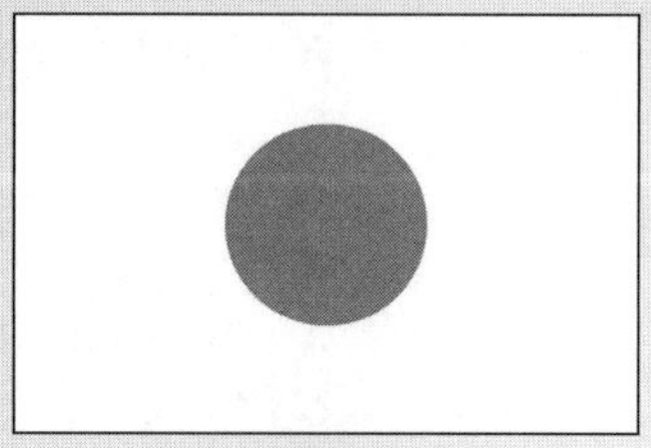

2 Kentaro's from Japan.
He's **J**__________**e**.

3 Emma's from the UK.
She's **B**__________**h**.

4 Bianca's from Brazil.
She's **Br**__________**n**.

5 Jacek's from Poland.
He's **P**__________**h**.

6 Mei-ling's from China.
She's **Ch**__________**e**.

7 Karl's from Germany.
He's **G**__________**n**.

8 William's from England.
He's **E**__________**h**.

9 Daniela's from Mexico.
She's **M**__________**n**.

10 Baba's from Egypt.
He's **E**__________**n**.

11 Derin's from Türkiye.
She's **T**__________**h**.

12 Mike's from the United States.
He's **Am**__________**n**.

13 Cédric's from Switzerland.
He's **Sw**__________**s**.

14 Adebayo's from Nigeria.
He's **N**__________**n**.

15 Juliette's from France.
She's **F**__________**h**.

2 PRONUNCIATION /dʒ/, /tʃ/, and /ʃ/

a **2.1 Listen and write the words in the chart.**

~~**Ch**inese~~ Egyp**ti**an Fren**ch** **G**erman **J**apanese **j**ust Ru**ss**ian tea**ch**er Turki**sh**

 1 **j**azz	 2 **ch**ess	 3 **sh**ower
	Chinese	

b **2.2 Listen and check. Then listen again and repeat the words.**

3 GRAMMAR verb *be* (plural): *we, you, they*

a **Write positive [+] and negative [−] sentences with *be*. Use contractions.**

1 we / from Spain ✓ Italy ✗
We're from Spain. We aren't from Italy.
2 you / teachers ✓ students ✗
________________.
3 they / Chinese ✓ Japanese ✗
________________.
4 we / from Mexico ✓ Brazil ✗
________________.
5 you / in class 3 ✓ class 2 ✗
________________.
6 they / from Egypt ✓ Türkiye ✗
________________.
7 she / in room 4 ✓ room 5 ✗
________________.
8 I / Polish ✓ British ✗
________________.

b **Write the sentences with pronouns. Use contractions.**

1 Juan and I are from Spain.
We're from Spain.
2 Sara and Mikel are in class 6.
________________.
3 Marina's on holiday.
________________.
4 Rodrigo's from Brazil.
________________.
5 Jake and I are here on business.
________________.
6 Toronto is in Canada.
________________.

c **Re-order the words to make questions.**

1 dogs they are your
Are they your dogs?
2 class in 1 are they
________________?
3 they Nigeria from are
________________?
4 Italian Fernanda is
________________?
5 in Zurich is Switzerland
________________?

d **Match the answers to the questions in c.**

a 4 Yes, she is.
b ___ No, they're in class 2.
c ___ No, they aren't.
d ___ Yes, it is.
e ___ Yes, they're from Abuja.

e **Answer the questions about your class.**

1 Are you British?
No, we aren't. We're ________________.
2 Where are you from?
________________.
3 What room are you in?
________________.

4 WORDS AND PHRASES TO LEARN

Complete the missing words in the conversations.

1 **A** Excuse me. Are ________ they ________ free ________?
B Yes, they are. Please sit down.
A Thanks.

2 **A** A________ y________ o________ h________?
B Yes, we are. We're from Spain.

3 **A** Your cappuccino.
B Thanks.
A H________ a n________ d________!

4 **A** Are you on business?
B No, we aren't. We're t________.
We're on holiday.

2B What number is the bus?

G *Wh-* and *How* questions with *be*
V numbers 11–100
P understanding numbers

1 GRAMMAR *Wh-* and *How* questions with *be*

a Complete the questions with a question word and *are* or *'s*.

1 **A** *Who's* __________ Freya Lawson?
B She's my English teacher.

2 **A** __________ the concert?
B It's on Monday.

3 **A** __________ she from?
B She's from Spain.

4 **A** __________ your phone number?
B It's 01632 960475

5 **A** __________ you from?
B I'm from Brazil.

6 **A** __________ Mari and Laura?
B They're on holiday in Boston.

7 **A** __________ Pedro?
B He's 27.

8 **A** __________ your address?
B It's 47 Bank Street.

9 **A** __________ you?
B I'm fine, thanks. And you?

b Complete the conversation. Write the questions.

A [1] *What's your name* __________?
B My name's Brian Halley.
A [2] __________?
B H-A-L-L-E-Y.
A Thank you. [3] __________?
B I'm from the United States.
A [4] __________?
B It's 64 Bond Street, New York City.
A Thank you. [5] __________?
B My phone number is 555-1105.
A [6] __________?
B It's b.halley@ukmail.com
A Thank you. [7] __________?
B I'm 23.
A [8] __________?
B No, I'm not. I'm single.

c Answer the questions about you.

1 What's your phone number?
____

2 What's your postcode?
____

3 Are you single?
____

4 What's your surname?
____

5 What's your address?
____

6 How old are you?
____

7 What's your email?
____

8 How do you spell your surname?
____

2 VOCABULARY numbers 11–100

a Complete the numbers.

1 20 t w e nt y
2 15 f __ __ t __ __ n
3 90 ni __ __ t __
4 70 s __ v __ nt __
5 12 t __ __ lv __
6 100 a hu __ __ r __ __
7 80 ei __ __ t __
8 11 e __ __ v __ __
9 40 fo __ t __
10 13 th __ r __ __ __ n
11 60 si __ t __

b Write the numbers.

1 forty-seven 47
2 nineteen ____
3 thirty-eight ____
4 fifty-nine ____
5 seventy-two ____
6 fourteen ____
7 ninety-one ____
8 sixteen ____
9 twenty-three ____
10 eighteen ____

3 PRONUNCIATION understanding numbers

a 2.3 Listen and complete the phone numbers.

1 0 __ 2 __ 7 __ __ 4 __ __ 3 __
2 __ 1 7 __ 9 __ __ 2 1 __ __
3 0 __ __ 3 5 __ 8 __ 1 __

b Listen again and repeat the phone numbers.

c 2.4 Listen and write the numbers.

1 17 London Road
2 I'm ____.
3 anne.davis____@mail.com
4 You're in room ____.
5 SW____ 4RJ

d Listen again and repeat the numbers.

4 WORDS AND PHRASES TO LEARN

Complete the missing words in the conversations.

1 **A** Who's ________ she________?
B Kaya.
A H________ o________ is she?
B She's 21.
A W________ c________ is she in?
B She's in my class.
A She's very g________-l________.

2 **A** Hi, Tom. H________ a________ y________?
B I'm f________, thanks.
A Th________ is Kaya.
B Nice to meet you.
C Nice to meet you, too. That's my bus. S________ y________ l________.

3 **A** Where are you from?
B Bournemouth.
A Where's Bournemouth?
B It's i________ t________ s________ of England.

3A Where's my phone?

G singular and plural nouns, *a* / *an*
V small things
P /z/ and /s/, plural endings

1 VOCABULARY small things

Complete the words.

1 watch

2 t__________

3 p__________

4 p__________

5 p__________

6 u__________

7 b__________

8 w__________

9 p__________

10 b________ c________

11 c__________

12 n__________

13 g__________

14 c__________

15 ID __________

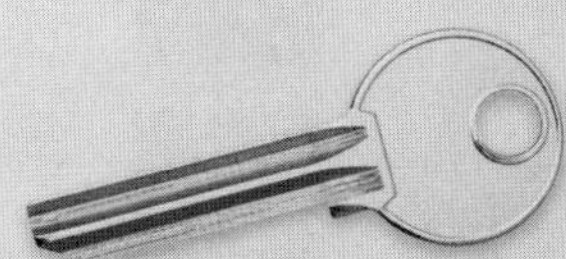

16 k__________

2 GRAMMAR singular and plural nouns, *a* / *an*

a Write *a* or *an*.

1 *a* camera
2 *an* umbrella
3 ____ book
4 ____ watch
5 ____ email
6 ____ country
7 ____ city
8 ____ key
9 ____ address
10 ____ laptop
11 ____ bank card

b Write the plurals of the words in **a**.

1 *cameras*
2 __________
3 __________
4 __________
5 __________
6 __________
7 __________
8 __________
9 __________
10 __________
11 __________

c Write questions and answers.

1 What is it ?
It's a dictionary .

2 ____________________?
____________________.

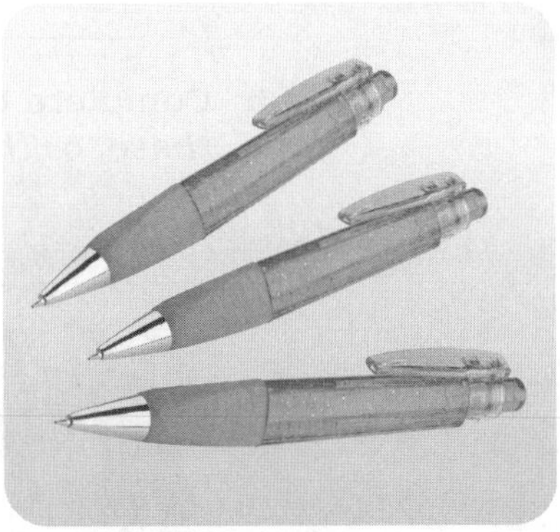

3 ____________________?
____________________.

4 ____________________?
____________________.

5 ____________________?
____________________.

6 ____________________?
____________________.

7 ____________________?
____________________.

8 ____________________?
____________________.

d What's in your bag? Write five things.

a wallet
____
____
____
____
____

3 PRONUNCIATION /z/ and /s/, plural endings

a 3.1 Listen and repeat the sounds and words.

 **z**ebra	1 name**s** bag**s**
 **s**nake	2 book**s** student**s**
/ɪz/	3 address**es** purs**es**

b 3.2 Listen and circle three words with /ɪz/.

pieces classes coats glasses laptops pencils phones wallets

c Listen again and repeat the words.

4 WORDS AND PHRASES TO LEARN

Complete the conversations with a phrase from the list.

~~Oh no~~ What are they What's in your bag Where are my glasses

1 **A** Where's your bag?
B Oh no ! It's in the car!

2 **A** ____________________?
B They're in your bag.

3 **A** Excuse me, sir. ____________________?
B I have a wallet, a book, and an umbrella.

4 **A** ____________________?
B They're bank cards.

Souvenirs

G *this / that / these / those*
V souvenirs
P /ð/, sentence rhythm

1 VOCABULARY souvenirs

Match the words in the list to the pictures.

~~cap~~ football shirt key ring mug
plate scarf teddy T-shirt

1 cap

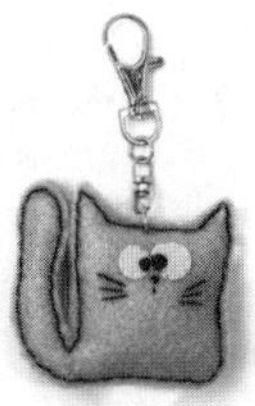

2 ______________

3 ______________

4 ______________

5 ______________

6 ______________

7 ______________

8 ______________

2 GRAMMAR *this / that / these / those*

a Re-order the words to make sentences or questions.

1 these bags are
These are bags.

2 is what that
______________________________?

3 book isn't this your
______________________________.

4 plates my those are
______________________________.

5 your are keys those
______________________________?

6 my aren't photos these
______________________________.

7 that friend is your
______________________________?

8 from where this is
______________________________?

b Complete the sentences with *this*, *that*, *these*, or *those*.

1 That's a lovely picture!

2 **A** Is ____________ a Manchester United shirt?
B No, it's Manchester City.

3 ____________ are £10.

4 **A** Are ________ your keys?
B Yes, they are. Thank you!

5 Look! ________'s Martin from our English class.

6 Wow. ________ are good glasses!

7 **A** I like ________ cap.
B Yes, it's very nice.

8 **A** Are ________ teddies £5?
B No, they're £10.

c **Complete the conversations with typical souvenirs from your country and the price.**

1 **A** Excuse me. What are those?
B They're *key rings*.
A How much are they?
B They're *€3.50*.

2 **A** Excuse me. What's that?
B It's a(n) ________.
A How much is it?
B It's ________.

3 **A** Excuse me. What are these?
B They're ________.
A How much are they?
B They're ________.

4 **A** Excuse me. What's this?
B It's a(n) ________.
A How much is it?
B It's ________.

3 PRONUNCIATION /ð/, sentence rhythm

a **3.3 Listen and complete the sentences.**

1 *This* is *my* *mother*.
2 ________ ________ over there?
3 ________ are my keys.
4 ________ are your ________.
5 Is ________ your ________?

b **Listen again and repeat the sentences. Copy the rhythm.**

4 WORDS AND PHRASES TO LEARN

Complete the missing words in the conversations.

1 **A** H*ow* m*uch* a*re* these key rings?
B They're €2.50.

2 **A** I________ this y________ phone?
B Oh yes, it is. Thank you very much.
A Y________ w________.

3 **A** Is that your bag th________?
B No, my bag's h________.

4 **A** H________ m________ i________ th________ mug?
B It's £5.00.

An orange juice, please

understanding prices, buying lunch **P** /ʊə/, /s/, and /k/

1 UNDERSTANDING PRICES

a Write the numbers.

1 *one* ______ cent

2 ______ dollars

3 ______ cents

4 ______ euros

5 ______ pence (p)

6 ______ pounds

b Complete the prices.

1 €75 seventy-five *euros* ______

2 £21.99 twenty-one ______ ninety-nine

3 $38.50 thirty-eight ______ and fifty cents

4 40p forty ______

5 €11.60 eleven ______ sixty

6 £2.50 two ______ fifty

c Write the prices.

1 *forty-five pounds*

2 ______

3 ______

4 ______

5 ______

6 ______

7 ______

8 ______

2 PRONUNCIATION /ʊə/, /s/, and /k/

a 3.4 Listen and circle the word with a different sound.

 **tou**rist	1 *(journalist)* **su**re **Eu**ropean
 **s**nake	2 pen**c**il pri**c**e **c**offee
 **k**ey	3 **c**ard **c**ent **c**amera

b Listen again and repeat the words.

c 3.5 Write the words in the chart. Listen and check. Then listen again and repeat the words.

~~city~~ ~~class~~ **c**lose ni**c**e pi**c**ture pen**ce**

 **s**nake	1 *city*
 **k**ey	2 *class*

3 BUYING LUNCH

a Read the menu and write the prices.

MENU

FOOD	DRINK
Steak or fish pie **£9.50**	Mineral water **£2.25**
Cheese, tuna, or chicken sandwiches **£5.75**	Orange juice **£3.60**
Burger **£7.99**	Coke / Diet Coke **£2.60**
Chicken salad **£8.20**	Coffee / Tea **£2.70**

1 **A** How much is a steak pie?
B It's £9.50.

2 **A** How much is a burger?
B It's ________.

3 **A** How much is a chicken salad?
B It's ________.

4 **A** How much is an orange juice?
B It's ________.

5 **A** How much is a coffee?
B It's ________.

b Complete the conversations.

a ~~Hi. A chicken salad and a Diet Coke, please.~~
b Here you are.
c How much is it?
d Thanks.
e Can I have a burger and an orange juice, please?
f Here's your change.
g Yes, a mineral water.
h No, thanks.
i Anything else?

1

Barman	Who's next?
Sally	1 Hi. A chicken salad and a Diet Coke, please.
Barman	Anything else?
Sally	2 ________
Barman	Ice and lemon with your drinks?
Sally	3 ________
Barman	There you go. That's £10.65.
Sally	4 ________
Barman	Thanks. Here's your change.
Sally	5 ________

2

Assistant	Can I help you?
Dan	Yes. 6 ________
Assistant	Of course. 7 ________
Dan	No, thanks.
Assistant	There you go.
Dan	Thanks. 8 ________
Assistant	$12.25.
Dan	Here you are.
Assistant	Thanks. 9 ________
Dan	Thank you. Have a nice day.

4 USEFUL PHRASES

Complete the missing words and phrases in the conversations.

1 **A** Seb! Hi, how are you?
B I'm fine, thanks.

2 **A** That's $12.75, please.
B Here you are.
A Thanks. H________ your ch________.

3 **A** C________ I h________ a cheese sandwich, please?
B Yes, of course. Anything else?

4 **A** H________ m________ is it?
B €8.70.

5 **A** We can have lunch together at the pub.
B Sure! Gr________ i________.

6 **A** A________ e________?
B And a tea, please.

This is my family

G possessive adjectives, possessive *'s*
V people and family
P /ʌ/, /æ/, and /ə/

1 VOCABULARY people and family

a Complete the chart.

singular	plural
boy	1 boys
2	girls
woman	3
man	4
5	friends
child	6
person	7

b Complete the sentences.

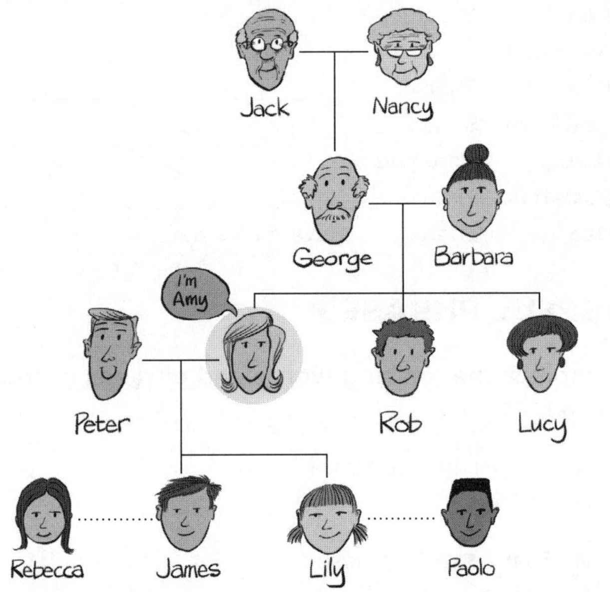

1 I'm Amy. I'm Peter's wife_______________.
2 George is my f_______________.
3 Peter's my h_______________.
4 Barbara's my m_______________.
5 George and Barbara are my p_______________.
6 Lily's my d_______________.
7 Rob's my br_______________.
8 James is my s_______________.
9 Rebecca is James's g_______________.
10 Lucy's my s_______________.
11 Paolo is Lily's b_______________.
12 Jack is my gr_______________.
13 Nancy is my gr_______________.
14 Jack and Nancy are my gr_______________.

2 GRAMMAR possessive adjectives, possessive *'s*

a Complete the chart.

subject pronoun	possessive adjective
I	1 my
2 you	your
he	3
4	her
it	5
6	our
you	7
8	their

b Complete the sentences with a possessive adjective.

1 That's my_______________ laptop!

2 This is _______________ daughter.

3 What's _______________ name?

4 Look at _______________ coat.

5 Here's _______________ coffee, sir.

6 This is _______________ new house.

7 It's an Italian restaurant. _______________ name is Luigi's.

8 _______________ names are Emily and Joel.

c Complete the sentences.

1 Carmen is Diego's sister.
Diego is *Carmen's brother* ______.

2 Charlotte is Peter's wife.
Peter is ______.

3 Mark is Angelina's brother.
Angelina is ______.

4 Richard is Maria's father.
Maria is ______.

5 Ana is Paulo's mother.
Paulo is ______.

6 Josh is Megan's husband.
Megan is ______.

7 Sarah is Michael's daughter.
Michael is ______.

8 Roberto is Luisa's son.
Luisa is ______.

d Look at the *'s* in the sentences. Tick (✓) Possessive or *is*.

	Possessive	***is***
1 Mark's wife is Brazilian.	✓	
2 Angela's on holiday.		✓
3 Those are Amy's cats.		
4 It's a great phone.		
5 This is my brother's room.		
6 Jennifer's in Paris.		
7 What's your name?		
8 Peter's son is twelve.		

e Think of five people. Who are they? Write a sentence about them.

Anna's my sister.
Ali's my friend's brother.

1 ______
2 ______
3 ______
4 ______
5 ______

3 PRONUNCIATION /ʌ/, /æ/, and /ə/

a 4.1 Listen and circle the word with a different sound.

 **u**p	1 br**o**ther M**o**nday (ph**o**ne) S**u**nday
 **u**p	2 s**o**n Th**ur**sday h**u**sband m**o**ther
 c**a**t	3 f**a**mily n**a**me th**a**nks s**a**ndwich
 comput**er**	4 m**e**n fath**er** childr**e**n wom**a**n

b Listen again and repeat the words.

4 WORDS AND PHRASES TO LEARN

Complete the conversations with a phrase from the list.

Be good ~~Come in~~ in my phone Let's order pizza on the table What a lovely card

1 **A** Hello, Billy! *Come in* ______.
B Thank you.

2 **A** Where's your phone?
B It's ______.

3 **A** What's Poppy's number?
B Just a minute. It's ______.

4 **A** Freddie, this is Ella. She's your babysitter today. ______.
B OK, Mum.

5 **A** ______.
B Good idea. I love pizza.

6 **A** ______!
B It's from my sister.

4B The right car for me

Ⓖ adjectives
Ⓥ colours and common adjectives
Ⓟ /ɑː/ and /ɔː/, linking

1 VOCABULARY colours and common adjectives

a Complete the colours with the missing vowels.

1 My car is bl_u_ _e_.
2 Her umbrella is bl__ck.
3 His bag is br__wn.
4 Gabriel's T-shirt is r__d.
5 The board is wh__t__.
6 Their house is gr__ __n.
7 Amelia's coat is y__ll__w.
8 His cap is __r__ng__.

b Complete the sentences with the opposite of the bold word.

1 Our house isn't **small**.
It's _big_______________.
2 My car isn't **fast**.
It's ________________.
3 Yulia's phone isn't **cheap**.
It's ________________.
4 His laptop isn't **new**.
It's ________________.
5 Tim's name isn't **long**.
It's ________________.
6 Their teacher isn't **bad**.
She's ________________.
7 My car isn't **clean**.
It's________________.
8 My cat isn't **ugly**.
It's ________________.
9 This exercise isn't **easy**.
It's ________________.

c Complete the words.

1 That house is very o_ld_________!

2 Is this bag e___________?

3 This book is very l___________.

4 The English test is d___________.

5 Oliver's car is very c___________.

6 Those phones are ch___________.

2 GRAMMAR adjectives

a Re-order the words to make sentences.

1 I a car have blue

I have a blue car.

2 a it's expensive camera very

______.

3 good they're children very

______.

4 a cheap that's phone

______.

5 has a my house red door

______.

6 a day it's beautiful

______.

7 a new tablet I have

______.

8 watch this nice is a

______.

b Rewrite the sentences.

1 The car is very slow.

It's a very slow car.

2 These exercises are very easy.

They're ______.

3 This film is very long.

It's a ______.

4 The windows are green.

They're ______.

5 Those umbrellas are very big.

They're ______.

6 That phone is old.

It's an ______.

7 The people are nice.

They're ______.

8 The dictionary is Spanish.

It's a ______.

3 PRONUNCIATION /ɑː/ and /ɔː/, linking

a 4.2 Listen and circle the word with a different sound.

 car	1 fast (flag) father
 horse	2 old short small
 car	3 passport family glasses
 horse	4 brown tall daughter

b Listen again and repeat the words.

c 4.3 Listen and write the phrases.

1 ______
2 ______
3 ______
4 ______
5 ______

d Listen again and repeat the phrases.

4 WORDS AND PHRASES TO LEARN

Complete the conversation with phrases from the list.

Come with me easy to park I love it in my opinion I prefer that red car ~~Is the car for you~~

A [1] Is the car for you?
B No, it's for my daughter.
C Yes, it's for me. It's my birthday.
A What about this green car here? It's small and it's [2] ______.
B Well, [3] ______, it's perfect for you.
C But I don't like green. [4] ______.
B The red one? That's a sports car!
C Yes, but it's my birthday and [5] ______! It's a beautiful car. How much is it?
A [6] ______, madam.

5A My favourite meal

G present simple [+] and [–]: *I, you, we, they*
V food and drink
P word stress, /dʒ/ and /g/

1 VOCABULARY food and drink

a Match the words from the list to the pictures.

bread butter cereal cheese coffee
eggs ~~fruit~~ rice sugar yogurt

1 *fruit*

2 ____________

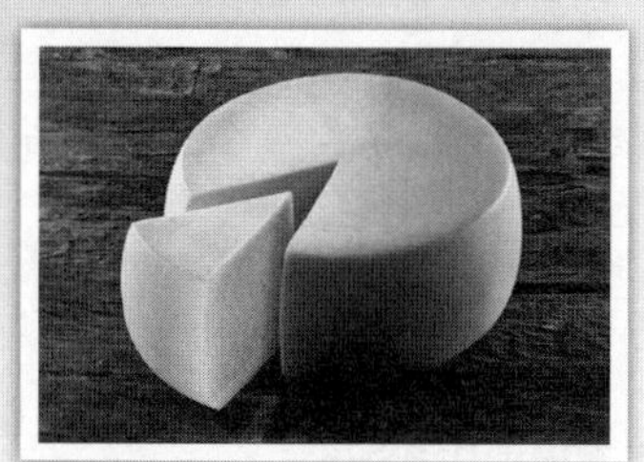

3 ____________

4 ____________

5 ____________

6 ____________

7 ____________

8 ____________

9 ____________

10 ____________

b What do they have for dinner? Complete the words.

1 f *i* *s* h
2 s *a* *l* *a* d
3 t __ a

4 p ___ a
5 v __________ s
6 m __ k

7 m __ t
8 p ________ s
9 w ___ r

10 a s ________ h
11 ch ________ e
12 or ____ e j ____ e

2 PRONUNCIATION /dʒ/ and /g/

a 5.1 Listen and under<u>line</u> the stressed syllable.

<u>cer</u>|e|al po|ta|toes vege|ta|bles
cho|colate break|fast sand|wich yo|gurt

b Listen again and repeat the words.

c 5.2 Listen and (circle) the word with a different sound.

 jazz	1 (get) orange juice
 girl	2 eggs Japan sugar
 jazz	3 sausages green vegetables
 girl	4 good yogurt Germany

d Listen again and repeat the words.

3 GRAMMAR present simple [+] and [–]: *I, you, we, they*

a Complete the sentences with the [+] or [–] of the verb in brackets.

1 My friends *don't eat* healthy food. ([–] eat)
2 I ______________ breakfast at home. ([–] have)
3 You ______________ a lot of water. ([+] drink)
4 I ______________ fish. ([+] like)
5 I ______________ coffee in the afternoon. ([–] drink)
6 We ______________ a salad for lunch. ([+] have)
7 I don't drink tea because I ______________ it. ([–] like)
8 My children ______________ a lot of fruit. ([+] eat)

b Complete the texts with the correct form of the verbs from the list.

drink ~~have~~ not have not like

I'm Amélie, and I'm from France. During the week, I [1] *have* breakfast in a café. I [2] ______________ a big breakfast, just a croissant. And I [3] ______________ hot chocolate. I [4] ______________ tea or coffee.

eat not drink not have

My name is Laszlo and I'm from Hungary. I [5] ______________ breakfast with my family during the week, but at weekends we sit down together. We [6] ______________ a very big breakfast: eggs, cheese, meat, and bread. I [7] ______________ coffee, so I have tea.

c What's your favourite meal of the day? Where do you have it? What food and drink do you have?

My favourite meal of the day is

4 WORDS AND PHRASES TO LEARN

Complete the missing words in the sentences.

1 I don't eat breakfast because I'm not h*ungry* in the morning.
2 Some doctors and scientists think breakfast is an i______________ meal.
3 Breakfast is my f______________ meal.
4 I have lunch e______________ – at 12.00.
5 I sometimes have breakfast i______________ a c______________.
6 Rice, fish, and miso soup is a tr______________ breakfast in Japan.
7 I usually have breakfast a______________ h______________.

5B A very long flight

G present simple [?]: *I, you, we, they*
V common verb phrases 1
P /w/ and /v/, sentence rhythm and linking

1 GRAMMAR present simple [?]: *I, you, we* and *they*

a Complete the interview with the questions.

Are you married? What airline do you work for?
Do you have children? ~~What's your name?~~
Do you like your job? Where are you from?

Interview with
a flight attendant

1 *What's your name?*
My name's Lucas.

2 ______________________________
I'm from Rio de Janeiro. It's a big, beautiful city.

3 ______________________________
Yes, I am. My wife's Italian. Her name is Celia.

4 ______________________________
Yes, we do. We have a little girl. Her name's Bianca. She's three.

5 ______________________________
I work for a Brazilian airline.

6 ______________________________
Yes, I do. I work with my friends, and I speak to a lot of new people every day. It's very interesting.

b Complete the questions.

1 **A** We don't live in a flat.
B *Do you live* ______________ in a house?

2 **A** I don't want a newspaper.
B ______________ a magazine?

3 **A** They don't like dogs.
B ______________ cats?

4 **A** I don't have a camera.
B ______________ a phone?

5 **A** I don't drink tea.
B ______________ coffee?

6 **A** We don't have breakfast.
B ______________ lunch?

7 **A** I don't need a new phone.
B ______________ tablet?

c Complete the conversation with *do* or *don't*.

Jon	1 *Do* ________ you have a car, Rachel?
Rachel	No, I 2 ________.
Jon	Oh. 3 ________ you work in London?
Rachel	Yes, I 4 ________. I work in a bank.
Waiter	Excuse me. 5 ________ you want a coffee?
Jon	Yes, please.
Waiter	And you?
Rachel	No, thanks. I 6 ________ like coffee.
Waiter	We have tea. 7 ________ you like tea?
Rachel	Yes, I 8 ________.
Waiter	OK. One coffee and one tea.

d **Answer the questions about you.**

1 Do you work or study?

____

2 Where do you work / study?

____

3 Do you have a car?

____

4 Do you like coffee?

____

2 VOCABULARY common verb phrases 1

Write the verbs.

drink eat go ~~have~~ have listen like live
need read speak study want watch work

1 *have* lunch

2 ____________ cats

3 ____________ milk

4 ____________ French

5 ____________ Mexican food

6 ____________ magazines

7 ____________ a new car

8 ____________ to Brazilian music

9 ____________ in a bank

10 ____________ in a house

11 ____________ TV in the evening

12 ____________ three dogs

13 ____________ German

14 ____________ to English classes

15 ____________ a coffee

3 PRONUNCIATION /w/ and /v/, sentence rhythm and linking

a **5.3 Listen and write the words in the correct column.**

witch	**v**ase

b **Listen again and repeat the words.**

c **5.4 Listen and complete the sentences.**

1 Do you *want* *a* sandwich?

2 I ____________ ____________ brother and ____________ ____________ teacher.

3 I ____________ ____________ ____________ house ____________ ____________ small city.

4 I ____________ ____________ ____________ ____________ TV.

d **Listen again and repeat the sentences. Copy the rhythm.**

4 WORDS AND PHRASES TO LEARN

Complete the conversations with a phrase from the list.

~~Can I see your passport and boarding pass, please~~ Do you want fish or pasta
keep the change What time do we arrive

1 **A** *Can I see your passport and boarding pass, please*?
B Yes, here you are.

2 **A** Excuse me. ______________________________?
B Fish, please.

3 **A** ______________________________?
B In 15 minutes.

4 **A** That's £4.75, please.
B Here you are – ______________________________.

3 Practical English
What time is it?

telling the time **V** the time, saying how you feel **P** /ɒ/, silent consonants

1 TELLING THE TIME

Complete the conversations.

1 **A** What *time* is it?
B It's *quarter* to eleven.

2 **A** It's ten to five. What __________ your train?
B __________ five fifteen.

3 **A** What time is __________?
B It's quarter __________ four.

4 **A** Hello. I'm __________ I'm late.
B You're two hours late – __________ 11.30!

2 VOCABULARY the time

a Complete the times.

1 It's *half* __________ past two.

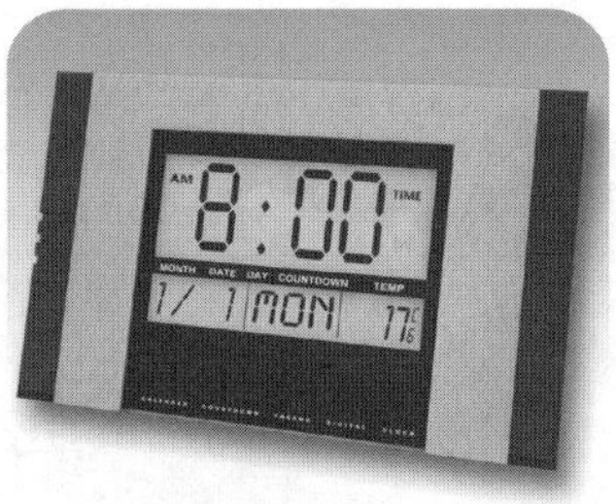

2 It's eight __________.

3 It's __________ past ten.

4 It's a __________ to six.

5 It's __________ past eleven.

6 It's __________ to one.

7 It's __________ past nine.

8 It's __________ to seven.

9 It's __________ past five.

10 It's __________ to twelve.

11 It's __________ past three.

12 It's __________ to four.

b 5.5 Listen and draw the times on the clocks.

1
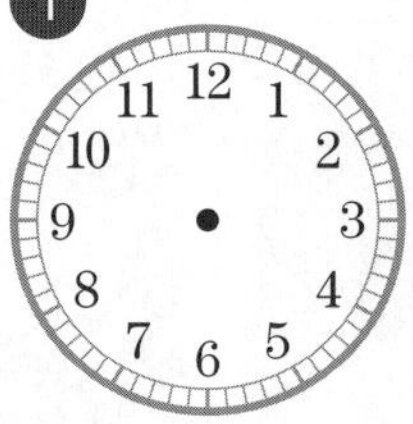

2
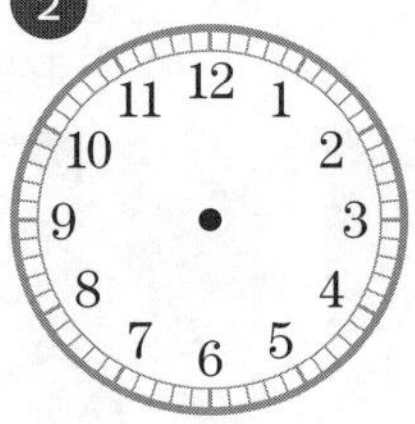

3

4
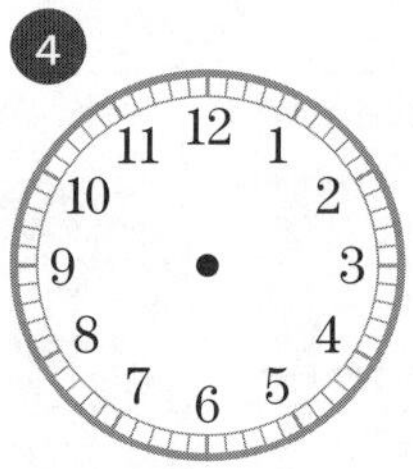

5

6

3 PRONUNCIATION /ɒ/, silent consonants

a 5.6 **Listen and circle the word with a different sound.**

/ɒ/	1 wh**a**t (sm**a**ll) h**o**t
	2 m**o**ther s**o**rry n**o**t
	3 **O**xford c**o**ffee s**o**n
	4 w**a**tch **o**ld **o**range
	5 l**o**ng w**a**nt n**o**w

b **Listen again and repeat the words.**

c 5.7 **Listen and cross out the silent consonants in these words.**

1 half
2 hour
3 know
4 listen
5 two
6 Wednesday
7 what
8 write

d **Listen again and repeat the words.**

4 VOCABULARY saying how you feel

Complete the sentences.

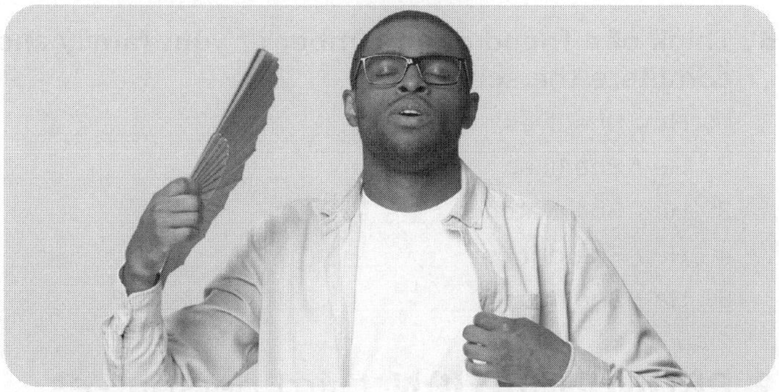

1 He's *hot* ______.

2 He's ______.

3 She's ______. 4 She's ______.

5 He's ______.

5 USEFUL PHRASES

Complete the missing words and phrases in the conversation.

A Hi, Adam. I'm [1]r*eally* ______ s*orry* ______ I'm late. What time's the film?
B [2]D______ w______. It's OK – it's at half past seven. It's only ten past seven.

***

A [3]W______ a gr______ film!
B Yes – fantastic! Do you want to go to the pub now?
A But it's half past ten. It's [4]l______ and I'm [5]t______.
B [6]C______ o______. I know a really good pub near here.
A Oh, OK. [7]L______ g______.

6A Old friends?

G present simple: *he, she, it*
V jobs and places of work
P third person *-es*, sentence rhythm

1 GRAMMAR present simple: *he, she, it*

a Look at the chart and complete the sentences.

	Amy	Luis
live in a big city	✗	✓
like cats	✓	✗
listen to pop music	✓	✗
speak French	✗	✓
drink tea	✗	✓

1 Amy *doesn't live* ________ in a big city.
2 She ________________ cats.
3 She ________________ to pop music.
4 She ________________ French.
5 She ________________ tea.
6 Luis ________________ in a big city.
7 He ________________ cats.
8 He ________________ to pop music.
9 He ________________ French.
10 He ________________ tea.

b Complete the text with the correct form of the verbs in brackets.

Kate's from Ireland, and she's an English teacher in Türkiye. She [1] *lives* ________ (live) in Istanbul, and she [2] ________________ (work) in a language school in the centre of the city. She [3] ________________ (not work) at the weekends because the school is closed. Kate [4] ________________ (like) Istanbul, but she [5] ________________ (not speak) Turkish very well. She [6] ________________ (have) a Turkish class in the morning, and she [7] ________________ (study) in the evening on her computer. She [8] ________________ (watch) TV at home, but she [9] ________________ (not understand) very much. She [10] ________________ (think) Türkiye is a fantastic country, and she [11] ________________ (not want) to go home.

c Complete the conversation with *do, does, don't,* or *doesn't*.

Mike Hello, I'm Mike.
Sarah Hi, I'm Sarah.
Mike What [1] *do* ________ you do, Sarah?
Sarah I'm a journalist.
Mike [2] ________________ you work for a newspaper?
Sarah No, I [3] ________________. I work for a magazine.
Mike Where [4] ________________ you work?
Sarah I work in different places. From home, in the office, in the street...
Mike [5] ________________ you like your job?
Sarah Yes, I [6] ________________. It's really interesting.
Mike Where [7] ________________ you live?
Sarah I have a very small flat in the centre of the city.
Mike [8] ________________ you have brothers and sisters?
Sarah Yes, I have one brother.
Mike What [9] ________________ he do?
Sarah He works in a shop.
Mike [10] ________________ he have a flat?
Sarah No, he [11] ________________. He lives with our parents.

d Think of a friend or a member of your family and complete the sentences.

1 He / She lives in ________________________.
2 He / She likes ________________________.
3 He / She watches ________________________.
4 He / She drinks ________________________.
5 He / She has ________________________.

2 PRONUNCIATION third person *-es*

a 6.1 Listen and circle four more words with /ɪz/ and write them in the chart.

closes does eats finishes has goes likes listens lives loves reads relaxes speaks teaches wants watches works

/ɪz/	*closes*

b Listen again and repeat the words.

3 VOCABULARY jobs and places of work

a Complete the jobs.

1 t*eache*______r

2 d______r

3 n______e

4 s______s a______t

5 f______y w______r

6 t______i d______r

7 p______e o______r

8 j______t

9 w______r

10 r______t

11 l______r

12 c______f

b Complete the sentences.

1 A factory worker works in a f*actory*______.
2 A writer works from h______.
3 A teacher works in a sc______.
4 A waiter works in a r______.
5 A police officer works in the st______.
6 A nurse works in a h______.
7 A sales assistant works in a sh______.
8 A receptionist works in a hotel or an o______.

4 PRONUNCIATION sentence rhythm

a 6.2 Listen and complete the conversations.

1 **A** What *does* ______ *she* ______ do?
B ______ ______ journalist.
A ______ ______ like her job?
B Yes, ______ ______.

2 **A** What ______ ______ do?
B ______ ______ waiter.
A Where ______ ______ work?
B ______ ______ in a café.

b Listen again and repeat the sentences. Copy the rhythm.

5 WORDS AND PHRASES TO LEARN

Complete the conversations with a word or phrase from the list.

Because   Great to see you   ~~He's married to Lisa~~
I love your shoes   intelligent   What does she do

1 **A** Who's that man with grey hair?
B That's Enzo. *He's married to Lisa*______.

2 **A** Lisa, Karl, hi! ______.
B Hello, Max. You too.

3 **A** ______ – they're beautiful!
B Thank you – they're new.

4 **A** ______?
B She's a nurse.

5 **A** Who's that with you?
B It's Diane, the ______ student in my class.

6 **A** Why do you get up at 5.30?
B ______ I start work at 6.30.

6B Good morning, goodnight

G adverbs of frequency
V a typical day
P /j/ and /juː/, sentence rhythm

1 VOCABULARY a typical day

a Complete the verb phrases.

1 get ________ up

2 f________ work

3 g________ shopping

4 h________ a shower

5 d________ housework

6 m________ dinner

7 w________ TV

8 g________ to bed

b Write the words in the chart.

~~a bath~~ a coffee breakfast dinner ~~home~~
lunch to bed to school to the gym to work

have	go
a bath	home

c Complete the text with the correct verbs.

do ~~finish~~ get up go (x4) have (x3) watch

I'm Hannah, and I'm a nurse. I work at night and I sleep during the day. I [1] finish ________ work at eight o'clock in the morning, and then I [2] ________ home and I [3] ________ to bed. I [4] ________ at about four o'clock in the afternoon, and I [5] ________ some cereal and orange juice for breakfast. Then I [6] ________ shopping and I [7] ________ the housework or [8] ________ TV. At seven o'clock in the evening I [9] ________ a shower, and I [10] ________ dinner before I [11] ________ to work again.

2 PRONUNCIATION /j/ and /juː/, sentence rhythm

a 6.3 Listen and tick (✓) the words which have the /j/ sound.

1 yellow ✓
2 factory ✗
3 young
4 yogurt
5 ugly
6 easy
7 boy
8 your
9 grey
10 yes

b Listen again and repeat the words.

c 6.4 Listen and tick (✓) the words which have the /juː/ sound.

1 usually ✓
2 umbrella ✗
3 study
4 student
5 music
6 number
7 beautiful
8 juice
9 newspaper
10 hurry

d Listen again and repeat the words.

e 6.5 **Listen and complete the sentences.**

1 I start work *at* __________ nine *in* __________ *the* __________ morning.

2 She __________ __________ coffee __________ __________ quarter __________ ten.

3 They __________ __________ sandwich __________ __________ café.

4 __________ finish work __________ six thirty.

5 __________ __________ housework __________ __________ weekend.

6 __________ watches TV __________ __________ evening.

f **Listen again and repeat. Copy the rhythm.**

3 GRAMMAR adverbs of frequency

a **Rewrite the sentences. Use the words in brackets.**

1 I get up early. (always)
I always get up early __________.

2 Yasmin goes to school by bus. (usually)
__________.

3 You do housework. (never)
__________.

4 They have fish for dinner. (sometimes)
__________.

5 Andy has lunch at home. (always)
__________.

6 I watch TV in the morning. (never)
__________.

7 We go shopping at the weekend. (sometimes)
__________.

8 They have coffee for breakfast. (usually)
__________.

b **Look at the chart and complete the sentences.**

✓✓✓✓✓ = *always* ✓✓✓ = *usually* ✓ = *sometimes* ✗ = *never*	 **Diego**	 **Jen**
go to the gym	✗	✓✓✓✓✓
read magazines	✓	✓✓✓
watch football on TV	✓✓✓✓✓	✓
get up early	✓✓✓	✗

1 Diego *never goes* __________ to the gym.

2 He __________ magazines.

3 He __________ football on TV.

4 He __________ early.

5 Jen __________ to the gym.

6 She __________ magazines.

7 She __________ football on TV.

8 She __________ early.

c **Write about your typical evening. Use adverbs of frequency.**

I always make dinner for my family. We usually eat at 7.00.

____

____

____

____

4 WORDS AND PHRASES TO LEARN

Complete the conversations with a word or phrase from the list.

~~Are you a morning person~~ every morning feel tired
He gets up at about 8.00 on the way to work
What time do you get up

1 **A** *Are you a morning person* __________?
B Yes, I get up at 6.00 every day.

2 **A** __________?
B I usually get up at about 9.30. I don't get up early.

3 **A** What time does Harry get up?
B __________.

4 **A** What do you do __________?
B I usually read a magazine on the bus.

5 **A** What do you have for breakfast?
B I have cereal and orange juice __________.

6 **A** Why do you go to bed at 8.30? It's very early.
B Because I always __________ after work.

7A At the weekend

G word order in questions: *be* and present simple
V common verb phrases 2: free time
P /w/, /h/, /eə/, and /aʊ/

1 VOCABULARY common verb phrases 2: free time

a Look at the pictures. Complete the questions.

1 Do you d*o*__________ sp*ort*__________?
2 Do you g__________ o__________ on a Friday night?
3 Do you go for a w__________ in the mountains?
4 Do you pl__________ c__________ g__________ after school?
5 Do you tr__________ a lot?
6 Do you pl__________ the p__________?
7 Do you r__________ after dinner?
8 Do you pl__________ t__________?
9 Do you m__________ fr__________ in a café at the weekend?
10 Do you sw__________?
11 Do you usually st__________ at h__________ in the evening?
12 Do you g__________ to the b__________ in the summer?

b Answer the questions in **a** about you.

1 ____________________.
2 ____________________.
3 ____________________.
4 ____________________.
5 ____________________.
6 ____________________.
7 ____________________.
8 ____________________.
9 ____________________.
10 ____________________.
11 ____________________.
12 ____________________.

2 GRAMMAR word order in questions: *be* and present simple

a Re-order the words to make questions.

1 where from is Alberto
Where is Alberto from?

2 how old our teacher is
_______________?

3 where does work your brother
_______________?

4 does speak French Emma
_______________?

5 have a big family do you
_______________?

6 is from Italy your girlfriend
_______________?

7 what time does go to work she
_______________?

8 are on holiday Oscar and Julia
_______________?

b Circle the correct question word.

1 **A** *Where* / *What* / *When* does your brother live?
B In São Paulo.

2 **A** *Where* / *When* / *What* do you usually have for breakfast?
B Cereal, fruit, and coffee.

3 **A** *How* / *Who* / *What* do you spell your last name?
B G-A-R-C-I-A.

4 **A** *What* / *When* / *Who* do you do housework?
B On Sunday morning.

5 **A** *How* / *When* / *Where* do you go to school?
B By bus.

6 **A** *How* / *How old* / *What* are your children?
B Jamal's four and Leyla's seven.

c Complete the questions with *is*, *are*, *do*, or *does*.

1 *Are* you good at sport?
2 When ________ you usually meet friends?
3 ________ your sister married?
4 ________ your husband play computer games?
5 How old ________ you?
6 How ________ your girlfriend travel to work?
7 Where ________ your teacher from?
8 ________ you have lunch at work?

3 PRONUNCIATION /w/, /h/, /eə/, and /aʊ/

a 7.1 Listen and circle the word with a different sound.

	**h**ouse	1 **h**ome **wh**at **h**ousework
	**h**ouse	2 **wh**o **h**oliday **wh**en
	**w**itch	3 **w**eekend s**w**im n**ow**
	ch**air**	4 h**ere** th**ere** wh**ere**
	**ow**l	5 m**ou**ntains h**ow** wind**ow**

b Listen again and repeat the words.

4 WORDS AND PHRASES TO LEARN

Complete the conversations with a word from the list.

~~definitely~~ depends exciting fan less

1 **A** What's the date today? Is it the 4th?
B Yes, *definitely* – it's my birthday!

2 **A** Where's Sean?
B He's at the football. He's a real Manchester City ________.

3 **A** When do you usually go shopping?
B It ________. Friday afternoon or Saturday morning.

4 **A** Do you do the same thing every evening?
B More or ________ – I have dinner and then I watch TV.

5 **A** Can you help me with the housework on Saturday morning?
B OK, but after lunch I want to do something fun and ________.

7B Lights, camera, action!

G imperatives, object pronouns: *me*, *him*, etc.
V kinds of film
P sentence rhythm

1 GRAMMAR imperatives, object pronouns: *me*, *him*, etc.

a Complete the conversations with a [+] or [–] imperative from the list.

buy eat go listen open ~~relax~~ sit use ~~watch~~ worry

1 **A** We need to hurry.
B [+] *Relax*________. We have time.

2 **A** Is that film good?
B No, it isn't. [–] *Don't watch*________ it.

3 **A** I'm tired.
B [+] __________ to bed. It's late.

4 **A** Is that a good phone?
B No, it isn't. [–] __________ it.

5 **A** Is that pasta for me?
B No, it isn't. [–] __________ it.

6 **A** Can I come in?
B Yes, of course.
[+] Please __________ down.

7 **A** Is this milk OK?
B No, it isn't. [–] __________ it.

8 **A** [+] __________ your books on page 32.
B Sorry, which page?

9 **A** Am I late?
B [–] No, __________. The lesson starts in five minutes.

10 **A** [+] __________ to me. This is very important.
B OK. What is it?

b Complete the sentences with an object pronoun.

1 I always say hello to Ryan, but he never talks to *me*________.
2 Emily loves her boyfriend, but I don't think he loves __________.
3 We go to my parents' house every weekend, but they never visit __________.
4 You often make dinner for me, but I never cook for __________.
5 I like the people I work with, but I never go out with __________.
6 My grandmother has a piano, but she never plays __________.
7 I know Jessica's husband, but I don't like __________.
8 Where are my glasses? I need __________ to read the newspaper.

c Complete the stories with a subject or object pronoun.

Three famous love stories in films

Ghost

Molly loves Sam and Sam loves Molly, but he never says 'I love [1] *you*________'. Sam dies, and now [2] __________ is a ghost. He watches Molly every day, but she can't see [3] __________. Sam meets a woman who is a psychic, and he uses [4] __________ to speak to Molly ...

My Fair Lady

Eliza Doolittle is a poor girl who sells flowers and Henry Higgins is a university professor. He teaches [5] __________ to speak English 'like a princess'. She falls in love with [6] __________, but he just thinks [7] __________ is an interesting student. She is angry and leaves [8] __________ ...

Titanic

17-year-old Rose is on a ship travelling from the UK to the the USA with her mother and a man called Cal Hockley. Her family want Rose to marry Cal because [9] __________ is rich, but on the ship she meets a poor artist, Jack Dawson, and falls in love with [10] __________. But one night, the ship hits an iceberg ...

2 VOCABULARY kinds of film

a Write the kinds of film.

1 an a*ction* __________ film
2 a c__________
3 a dr__________
4 a sc__________ f__________ film
5 a w__________
6 a h__________ film
7 an an__________

b Answer the questions about you.

1 What kinds of film do you like?
____
2 What's your favourite film?
____
3 Do you have a favourite TV series? What is it?
____
4 Who's your favourite actor?
____

3 PRONUNCIATION sentence rhythm

a 7.2 Listen and complete the sentences.

1 Do you *like* *Daniel* *Craig*?
2 __________, I __________.
3 I __________ him a __________.
4 I __________ he's __________.
5 Do you __________ __________ __________?
6 __________, I __________.
7 I __________ __________ them.
8 I __________ __________.

b Listen again and repeat. Copy the rhythm.

4 WORDS AND PHRASES TO LEARN

Complete the conversations with a phrase from the list.

~~be quiet~~ don't cry Don't move don't say anything I don't remember What about

1 **A** Shh – *be quiet*. I can't hear the teacher.
B Sorry...

2 **A** I need to talk to you.
B __________? I'm very busy!

3 **A** Sam, do you know what Jin's sister's name is?
B Sorry, __________.

4 **A** It's OK – __________. I can help you find your mum.
B Thank you.

5 **A** __________! There's a snake over there.
B A snake? I can't see a snake.

6 **A** Do you know that Otto has a new girlfriend?
B Yes, but __________ to his friends. It's a secret.

4 Practical English
What's the date?

saying the date, talking on the phone **V** months, ordinal numbers **P** /θ/

1 VOCABULARY months

Complete the months with the missing vowels.

1 J *a* n *u* *a* ry
2 F ___ br ___ ___ ry
3 M ___ rch
4 Apr ___ l
5 M ___ y
6 J ___ n ___
7 J ___ ly
8 A ___ g ___ st
9 S ___ pt ___ mb ___ r
10 Oct ___ b ___ r
11 N ___ v ___ mb ___ r
12 D ___ c ___ mb ___ r

2 VOCABULARY & PRONUNCIATION ordinal numbers, /θ/

a Complete the ordinal numbers.

1 2nd s *e c o n d*
2 20th tw ___ ___ ___ i ___ ___ ___
3 4th f ___ ___ r ___ ___
4 31st th ___ ___ ___ ___ ___ - f ___ ___ ___ ___ ___
5 5th f ___ f ___ ___
6 9th n ___ ___ t ___
7 3rd t ___ ___ ___ ___
8 12th tw ___ ___ ___ ___ ___ h
9 8th e ___ g ___ ___ ___
10 6th s ___ ___ ___ ___

b Write the next ordinal number.

1 first, *second* ______________
2 tenth, ______________
3 seventeenth, ______________
4 fourteenth, ______________
5 twenty-third, ______________
6 fifteenth, ______________

c 7.3 Listen and repeat the sentences. Copy the sounds and rhythm.

1 It's **Thursday** the **thirteenth**.
2 It's **three thousand dollars**.
3 I **think** it's **three thirty**.
4 His **third birthday's** on the **fifth**.

3 SAYING THE DATE

a Match the dates.

1	19/2	*f*	a	21st July
2	2/9	___	b	7th November
3	21/7	___	c	11th January
4	11/1	___	d	6th May
5	27/4	___	e	8th October
6	8/10	___	f	~~19th February~~
7	6/5	___	g	27th April
8	7/11	___	h	2nd September

b Cover a–h and just look at 1–8. Practise saying the dates. Remember to say *the* and *of*, for example, *the nineteenth of February*.

c Write the answers using the dates in brackets.

1 **A** What's the date today? (9/3)
B 9th March.

2 **A** What's the date on Saturday? (1/11)
B ______

3 **A** What's the date tomorrow? (2/6)
B ______

4 **A** When's your birthday? (18/12)
B ______

5 **A** When's your mother's birthday? (4/8)
B ______

6 **A** When's your best friend's birthday? (31/10)
B ______

d Answer 1–6 in **c** with your own answers.

1 ______
2 ______
3 ______
4 ______
5 ______
6 ______

4 TALKING ON THE PHONE

Put the conversation in the right order.

1 **A** Hello.
___ **A** Hi Gloria. Listen, now isn't a good time. I'm in a meeting. Can I call you later?
___ **A** Yes, it is. Who's that?
___ **A** OK. Speak later. Bye.
___ **B** This is Gloria Webster, from the New York office.
___ **B** Yes, no problem. Call me on this number this afternoon.
___ **B** Hello, is that Dave Freeman?

5 USEFUL PHRASES

Complete the conversations with a phrase from the list.

~~Call me on Monday at work~~ Is that
It's my dad's birthday This is for you
What's the date today

1 **A** We need to talk about our trip to Berlin.
B OK. Call me on Monday at work.

2 **A** ______?
B I think it's the 10th.

3 **A** ______ our new teacher?
B Yes. Her name's Mrs Mack.

4 **A** Isn't it the 5th today?
B No, it's the 6th. ______.

5 **A** ______. Happy birthday!
B Thank you.

8A Can I park here?

G *can / can't*
V more verb phrases
P *can / can't*: /ə/, /æ/, and /ɑː/, sentence rhythm

1 GRAMMAR *can / can't*

a **Complete the sentences with *You can / can't* and a verb from the list.**

change drink eat listen ~~park~~ swim

1 You can't park ______ here.
2 ______ here.
3 ______ money here.
4 ______ coffee here.
5 ______ food here.
6 ______ to music here.

b **Complete the conversations. Use *can*, the word in brackets, and a verb from the list.**

~~have~~ play read sit swim watch

1 **A** Can I have ______ an espresso, please? (I)
B Regular or large?

2 **A** ______? (we)
B No – the water's very cold today.

3 **A** ______ TV? (we)
B Finish your homework first.

4 **A** Excuse me. ______ here? (I)
B Sorry, no. That's my friend's seat.

5 **A** ______ golf on Saturday? (you)
B Yes. What time?

6 **A** Look. It's an email from Amina.
B Really? ______ it? (I)

2 PRONUNCIATION *can / can't*: /ə/, /æ/, and /ɑː/, sentence rhythm

a **8.1 Listen and choose the correct sound for *can / can't* in these sentences.**

1 Can I **help you**? a
2 **Where** can I **sit down**? ______
3 **Sorry**, I **can't**. ______
4 **Yes**, you **can**. ______
5 You can **learn** to **drive here**. ______
6 I **can't speak Polish**. ______

b **Listen again and repeat. Copy the rhythm.**

3 VOCABULARY more verb phrases

a Complete the phrases.

1 u*se*________ the i*nternet*________

2 t________ a ph________

3 h________ a c________

4 p________ by c________

5 ch________ m________

6 sw________

7 dr________

8 pl________ f________

9 u________ your ph________

10 p________

b Write things you *can* or *can't* do in your country in these places.

1 in a school
You ________________________.

2 at the beach
You ________________________.

3 in a museum
You ________________________.

4 in a supermarket
You ________________________.

5 in a coffee shop
You ________________________.

6 in a gym
You ________________________.

4 WORDS AND PHRASES TO LEARN

Complete the conversations with a phrase from the list.

a theory test   I'm free   ~~it's a total disaster~~
learn to drive   start the car   Yes, of course

1 **A** Can you go to Tara's party on Friday night?
B No, I need to study – *it's a total disaster*!

2 **A** When do you want to see the new James Bond film?
B ________________ on Friday night.

3 **A** Can I have another drink, please?
B ________________. Here you are.

4 **A** I want to ________________.
Do you know a good driving instructor?
B Yes, my neighbour! She's very good.

5 **A** Do you need to take ________________ to get a driving licence in your country?
B Yes, but it's very easy.

6 **A** Your practical test begins now.
Please ________________.
B Yes. Sorry, I'm very nervous.

I ❤ shopping

G *like / love / hate* + verb + *-ing*
V activities
P /ʊ/, /uː/, and /ŋ/, sentence rhythm

1 VOCABULARY activities

Write the activities.

1 r*eading*

2 b________ clothes

3 c________

4 g________ to the cinema

5 p________

6 c________

7 w________ TV series

8 fl________

9 c________

10 d________ y________

11 e________ o________

12 g________ for a walk

13 r________

14 sh________

15 s________

16 sl________

17 sw________

18 tr________

2 GRAMMAR *like / love / hate* + verb + *-ing*

a Complete the chart with the *-ing* form of the verbs in the list.

~~begin~~ ~~drive~~ get ~~listen~~ live make
play relax sit stop study write

+ *-ing*	~~e~~ + *-ing*	double consonant + *-ing*
listening	driving	beginning

b Complete the sentences with the *-ing* form of a verb from the list.

drive get listen live pay relax
~~sit~~ study take walk

1 Emma wants a new job because she hates sitting ______ in an office all day.
2 Darius likes ______ in a big city because there's a lot to do.
3 I hate ______ tests. I'm always very nervous.
4 My mother has a car, but she hates ______.
5 I want to learn Italian, but I don't like ______.
6 My brother loves ______ to music.
7 I don't like ______ cash. I prefer using cards.
8 We usually go to the Pyrenees for our holidays. We like ______ in the mountains.
9 I love ______ at home on a Sunday evening. I usually watch TV or read a book.
10 I don't like ______ up early. I always feel tired in the morning.

c Write sentences.

❤ = love ✓ = like ✗ = not like ✗✗ = hate

1 She / dance ❤
She loves dancing.
2 My brother / play tennis ✓
______
3 Lisa / live in the city ✗✗
______
4 I / make dinner for my family ❤
______
5 My dad / listen to classical music ✓
______
6 My children / get up early at the weekend ✗
______

d Write sentences about the activities you *love*, *like*, *don't like*, and *hate* doing.

I love going for a walk in the evening.
______
______
______
______

3 PRONUNCIATION /ʊ/, /uː/, and /ŋ/, sentence rhythm

a 8.2 Listen and write the words in the chart.

~~book~~ f**oo**d g**oo**d l**oo**k sch**oo**l s**oo**n t**oo**

 1 b**u**ll	 2 b**oo**t
book	

b 8.3 Listen and check. Then listen again and repeat the words.

c 8.4 Listen and repeat. Copy the sounds and the rhythm.

1 **cooking**
2 I **like cooking**.
3 **swimming**
4 Do you **like swimming**?
5 **reading**
6 I **love reading**.

4 WORDS AND PHRASES TO LEARN

Complete the missing words in the sentences.

1 We love walking in the mountains because it's very peaceful ______.
2 Let's stay at home this evening. The weather's h______. It's really cold.
3 Do you like travelling a______ or do you prefer going with someone else?
4 Soraya's always the first person to dance a______ p______.
5 My dad's a terrible singer, but he always sings v______ l______ in the shower.
6 My sister's really f______ of dogs, especially big ones.

9A What are they *really* doing?

G present continuous
V common verb phrases 2: travelling
P sentence rhythm

1 GRAMMAR present continuous

a Complete the chart with the *-ing* form of the verbs in the list.

~~buy~~ cook ~~cycle~~ give have ~~run~~ shop
swim travel use watch work

+ *-ing*	~~e~~ + *-ing*	double consonant + *-ing*
buying	cycling	running

b Complete the sentences with the verbs from a in the present continuous.

1 My brother's travelling ________ in South Africa at the moment.
2 ________ you ________ the internet?
3 They ________ in the sea.
4 Erica ________ in a marathon.
5 Lisa ________ to work because she has a new bike.
6 ________ he ________ in the office today?
7 They ________ TV at the moment.
8 She ________ a shower.
9 ________ you ________ those shoes? They're lovely, but they're very expensive.
10 Sami's in the kitchen. He ________.

2 PRONUNCIATION sentence rhythm

a 9.1 Listen and complete the sentences.

1 What ________ are you doing ________?
2 I'm ________ the ________.
3 ________ she ________?
4 She's ________ a ________ ________.
5 ________ are they ________?
6 They're ________ to the ________.

b Listen again and repeat. Copy the rhythm.

3 VOCABULARY common verb phrases 2: travelling

a Write the verbs.

1 g e t a taxi

2 b____ tickets

3 l____ the house

4 b___ presents

5 st___ in a hotel

6 r____ a car

7 p____ a suitcase

8 w____ sunglasses

9 c_____ a suitcase

10 ph____ home

11 a_______ at a hotel

12 w____ for a flight

b Write what the people are doing in **a**.

1 He's getting a taxi.
2 She's ____________
3 ____________
4 ____________
5 ____________
6 ____________
7 ____________
8 ____________
9 ____________
10 ____________
11 ____________
12 ____________

4 WORDS AND PHRASES TO LEARN

Complete the conversations with a word or phrase from the list.

Are you sure   box office   Have a good day   ~~in an hour~~   outside   towards

1 **A** Do you want to meet us for lunch after your class?
B Yes – great. See you in an hour in the canteen.

2 **A** Carlos is late again! The bus leaves at 10.00!
B Well, he's coming now. Look – he's walking ____________ us.

3 **A** Are you booking the train tickets?
B Yes. ____________ you want to leave at 6.00 a.m.? It's very early.

4 **A** I'm leaving now. See you this evening.
B Bye. ____________!

5 **A** Is it raining ____________?
B Yes, it is. Don't forget your umbrella.

6 **A** Where's Jenny?
B She's buying the cinema tickets at the ____________.

9B Watching and waiting

G present continuous or present simple?
V clothes
P /ɜː/, other vowel sounds

1 GRAMMAR present continuous or present simple?

a Circle the correct form.

[1]*I usually work* / *I'm usually working* in my office. Today [2]*I work* / *I'm working* at home.

[3]*We usually go* / *We're usually going* to school on Tuesday, but today is different. Our class [4]*visits* / *is visiting* an art gallery. [5]*We learn* / *We're learning* about Spanish painters.

[6]*We study* / *We're studying* outside today! [7]*We usually do* / *We're usually doing* our homework in the library, but today is different. [8]*We sit* / *We're sitting* in the sun and having a good time.

b Complete the conversations. Use the present simple or present continuous form of the verb in brackets.

1 **A** Hi, can you talk now?
B Sorry, I can't. I'm making ______ dinner. (make)

2 **A** ________ you ________ in Tokyo? (live)
B Yes, I do. It's a great city.

3 **A** How is Tracy's job?
B She's very busy. She ________ late again today. (work)

4 **A** Let's go to the pizza restaurant tonight.
B What about the Mexican restaurant? My husband ________ pizza. (not like)

5 **A** What time ________ your children ________ to bed? (go)
B Usually, about eight o'clock.

6 **A** Can I read your newspaper?
B Yes. I ________ it. (not read)

7 **A** Do you want to go out for a walk?
B Not now. It ________. (rain)

8 **A** Why ________ Tom ________ a suit? (wear)
B He has an important meeting at work today.

2 VOCABULARY clothes

a Write the words.

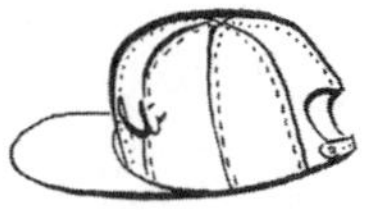

1 cap 2 ______ 3 ______ 4 ______

5 ______ 6 ______ 7 ______ 8 ______

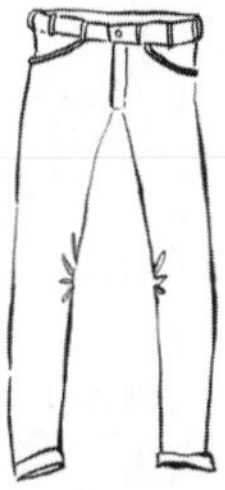
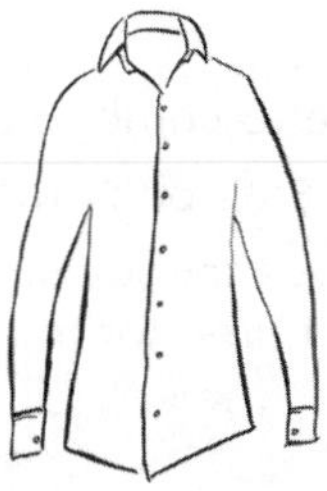

9 ______ 10 ______ 11 ______ 12 ______

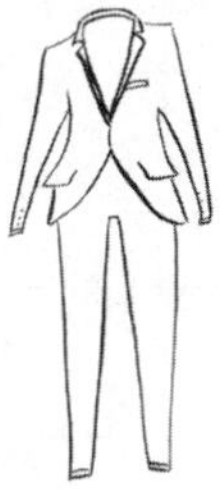
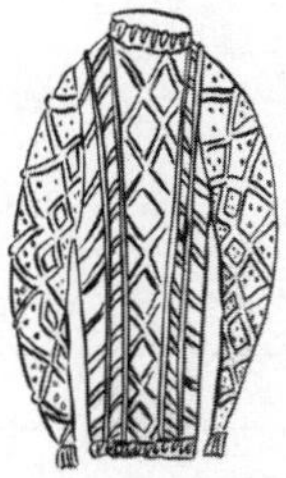

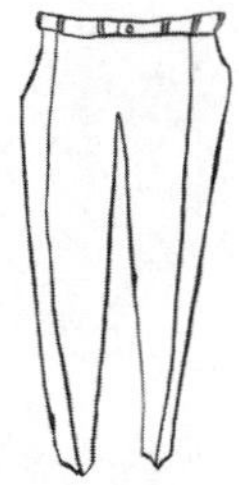

13 ______ 14 ______ 15 ______ 16 ______

b Answer the questions about you.

1 What are you wearing today?

______

2 What colours do you like wearing?

______

3 What clothes do you usually wear...?

- in the summer
- in the winter
- to work / school
- for a party

______

______

______

______

3 PRONUNCIATION /ɜː/, other vowel sounds

a 9.2 Listen and repeat the sound and words.

 bird	serve shirt skirt

b 9.3 Listen and circle three words with /ɜː/.

there third jeans quarter wear
word meeting girl chair

c Listen again and repeat the words.

d 9.4 Listen and circle the word with a different sound.

 egg	1 (jeans) sweater dress
 boot	2 suit trousers shoes
 cat	3 hat cap coat

e Listen again and repeat the words.

4 WORDS AND PHRASES TO LEARN

Complete the missing words in the sentences.

1 Ava is my colleague at work.
2 I a______ phone calls in the office.
3 My friend is a private i______.
4 I'm tired, and it's difficult to s______ awake.
5 My c______ pay me for my work.
6 I like my job. It's very s______.

5 Practical English
Would you like to come?

inviting and offering | P sentence rhythm

1 INVITING AND OFFERING

a Complete the conversations.

Are 'd It Let's like see sugar time What ~~Would~~

1 **A** [1]*Would* ________ you like to come to a basketball match on Saturday?
B What [2]________'s the match?
A [3]________'s at 7.30 at the sports centre.
B I'd love to. Thanks.
A Would you [4]________ to meet for a drink first?
B Yes, OK. [5]________ meet at 6.30 in the bar.
A OK, [6]________ you there.

2 **A** Hi John. [7]________ you hungry?
B No, but I [8]________ like a drink.
A [9]________ would you like to drink?
B A coffee, please.
A Milk and [10]________?
B Just milk, please.

b Complete the emails.

a No problem. How about dinner?
b My daughter goes to swimming lessons at 2.00.
~~c Would you like to come to my house for lunch on Saturday?~~
d Can you come at about 8.00?
e Yes, I'd love to come to dinner.
f See you at 8.00 on Saturday.
g Sorry! I'd love to, but Saturday lunchtime isn't a good time for me.

Hi Marta,
[1]*Would you like to come to my house for lunch on Saturday?*
Best wishes,
Angela

Hi Angela,
[2]________
[3]________
Marta

Hi Marta,
[4]________
[5]________
Angela

Hi Angela,
[6]________
[7]________
Love,
Marta

2 PRONUNCIATION sentence rhythm

a 9.5 **Listen and complete the sentences.**

1 Would you *like* ________ a *pizza* ________?
2 Would you ________ to ________ for ________?
3 Would you ________ ________ to ________?
4 Would you ________ to ________ to the ________?
5 Would you ________ to play ________?
6 Would you ________ ________ or a ________?

b Listen again and repeat. Copy the rhythm.

3 USEFUL PHRASES

Complete the conversations with a phrase from the list.

how about a coffee ~~I'd like to ask you something~~
Let's meet at half past six Yeah, I'd love to
Would you like a burger

1 **A** Hi, Zak. *I'd like to ask you something*.
Would you like to come to a party on Friday?
B Yes, I'd love to! Where is it?

2 **A** Would you like to come to the match with me on Saturday?
B ________________. What time does it start?

3 **A** ________________?
B No, thanks. I'm not very hungry.

4 **A** ________________ at the entrance to the cinema.
B OK. See you there.

5 **A** I don't want breakfast, thanks. I don't eat in the morning.
B Well, ________________?

4 WRITING an email

a **Read the email inviting you to do something. Circle the correct phrase.**

1*Hi / Good morning* (your name),

2*Would / Do* you like 3*to come / come* to dinner 4*in / on* Friday? 5*I'm inviting / I invite* Isabel too.

6*Can you come / Can come you* at 7.30? I love 7*cooking / cook* Chinese food. Do you like it?

See you on Friday (I hope!).

Love,

Elena

b Write a reply to the invitation.

____
____
____
____
____
____

10A A room with a view

G *there's a... / there are some...*
V hotels; *in, on, under*
P /ɪə/ and /eə/

1 VOCABULARY hotels

a Complete the words.

1 towe_____l

2 b_____h

3 s_____r

4 c_____d

5 f_____r

6 t_____e

7 b_____m

8 l_____p

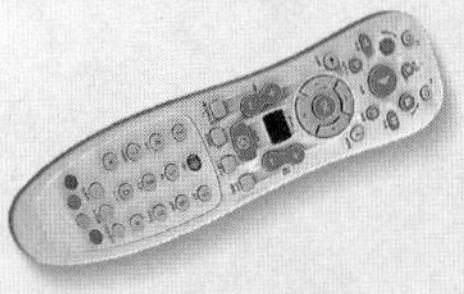

9 r_____e c_____l

10 p_____w

11 l_____t

12 b_____d

b Complete the sentences with the words from the list.

bar car park garden gift shop gym ~~lift~~ reception restaurant spa swimming pool

1 You can use the lift_____ to go upstairs.
2 You can swim in the _____.
3 You can have dinner in the _____.
4 You can buy keyrings in the _____.
5 You can sit outside in the _____.
6 You can do exercise in the _____.
7 You can park your car in the _____.
8 You can pay at _____.
9 You can buy drinks in the _____.
10 You can relax in the _____.

2 GRAMMAR *there's a... / there are some...*

a Look at the picture. Complete the sentences.

1 There's a_____ bed.
2 There are some_____ pillows.
3 _____ lamp.
4 _____ table.
5 _____ towels.
6 _____ chair.
7 _____ suitcase.
8 _____ books.

b Write negative [–] sentences.

1 There's a gym in the hotel.
There isn't a gym in the hotel_____.
2 There are some pillows in the cupboard.
_____.
3 There are some lamps in the room.
_____.
4 There's a restaurant on the first floor.
_____.
5 There's a swimming pool in the garden.
_____.

c Write questions and answers.

1 restaurants *Are there any restaurants?*
Yes, there are.
2 spa *Is there a spa?*
No, there isn't.
3 toilets ______________________
____
4 swimming pool ______________________
____
5 gift shops ______________________
____
6 lifts ______________________
____
7 gym ______________________
____
8 garden ______________________
____

d What is there in your classroom? Write sentences about the words in the list.

computer dictionaries pictures
TV board windows

There are some dictionaries.
____
____
____
____
____

3 PRONUNCIATION /ɪə/ and /eə/

a 10.1 Listen and circle the word with a different sound.

eə ch**air**	1 wh**ere** (h**ere**) th**ere**
eə ch**air**	2 b**ee**r th**ei**r **air**port
ɪə **ea**r	3 n**ea**r y**ea**r wh**ere**
ɪə **ea**r	4 rep**ai**r id**ea** w**e're**

b Listen again and repeat the words.

4 VOCABULARY *in, on, under*

Where's the remote control? Write sentences.

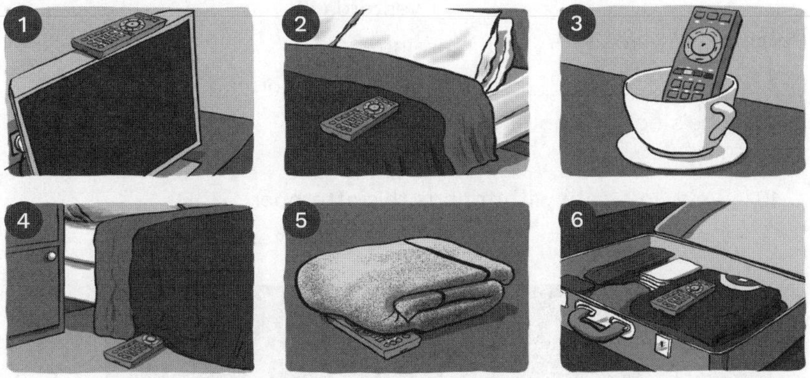

1 It's *on the television*.
2 It's ______________________.
3 It's ______________________.
4 ______________________.
5 ______________________.
6 ______________________.

5 WORDS AND PHRASES TO LEARN

Complete the conversation with the phrases from the list.

a boat trip a great view ~~a room for tonight~~ Enjoy your stay
on the second floor

A Hi. Do you have [1]*a room for tonight*?
B Let's check. Yes, we do. There's a room [2]______________________, but it doesn't have a bathroom.
A Is there a view of the lake?
B Yes, there is. There's [3]______________________ of the lake and the castle.
A OK, that's great.
B Breakfast is at 7.30, and here's some information about [4]______________________ on the lake. [5]______________________!

10B Where was he?

G past simple: *be*
V *in, on, at*
P *was* and *were*, sentence rhythm

1 GRAMMAR past simple: *be*

a Rewrite the sentences in the past.

1 I'm at work now.
I was at work yesterday.

2 They aren't at home today.
They weren't at home yesterday.

3 He's at a restaurant tonight.
__________ last night.

4 We aren't at school today.
__________ yesterday.

5 Are you at work now?
__________ last night?

6 She's at the airport this evening.
__________ yesterday evening.

7 Is he late today?
__________ yesterday?

8 I'm not in a hurry this morning.
__________ yesterday morning.

9 She's not in a hotel tonight.
__________ last night.

10 We're in a café with friends this afternoon.
__________ yesterday afternoon.

b Write questions and answers.

1 Picasso / a painter (✓)
Was Picasso a painter?
Yes, he was.

2 the Beatles / from the United States (✗)
Were the Beatles from the United States?
No, they weren't.

3 Nelson Mandela / American (✗)
__________?
__________.

4 Charlotte Brontë and Jane Austen / writers (✓)
__________?
__________.

5 Carmen Miranda / Brazilian (✓)
__________?
__________.

6 Monet and Matisse / musicians (✗)
__________?
__________.

7 Frida Kahlo / a musician (✗)
__________?
__________.

8 Steve Jobs and Thomas Edison / American (✓)
__________?
__________.

c Complete the conversations with *was* / *wasn't* or *were* / *weren't*.

1 **A** *Were* you at work last week?
B Yes, I *was*.

2 **A** Where __________ you last night?
B I __________ at a party.

3 **A** __________ your friend at school yesterday?
B No, she __________.

4 **A** __________ your parents on holiday last week?
B No, they __________.

5 **A** When __________ your brother in Beijing?
B He __________ there last year.

6 **A** __________ you at the museum yesterday?
B No, we __________.

2 VOCABULARY *in*, *on*, *at*

a **Where were these people yesterday? Write sentences with *in*, *at*, or *on* and a word from the list.**

bed car home kitchen park plane
restaurant street ~~train~~ work

1 She was on a train.

2 They ______.

3 ______.

4 ______.

5 ______.

6 ______.

7 ______.

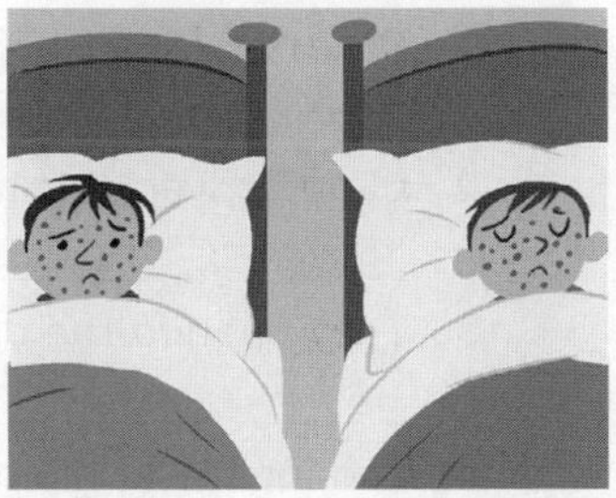

8 ______.

9 ______.

10 ______.

b **Answer the questions about you.**

1 Where were you at 6.30 yesterday morning?
I was in bed.

2 Where were you at 11.00 yesterday morning?
______

3 Where were you at 2.00 yesterday afternoon?
______

4 Where were you at 5.30 yesterday afternoon?
______

5 Where were you at 9.00 last night?
______

6 Where were you at 11.00 last night?
______

7 Where were you last Friday night?
______

8 Where were you last Saturday afternoon?
______

3 PRONUNCIATION *was* and *were*, sentence rhythm

a **10.2 Listen and complete the sentences.**

1 Where were you last night?
2 Were you at ______?
3 I was ______.
4 I ______ with my ______.
5 Were your ______ at ______?
6 My ______ was at ______.

b **Listen again and repeat. Copy the rhythm.**

4 WORDS AND PHRASES TO LEARN

Complete the sentences with the words from the list.

century ~~last~~ luxury secret
strong ~~suspect~~ together

1 There was a robbery in the bank last night and that man in the photo is a suspect.
2 There's a new ______ hotel in town – it's very expensive to stay there.
3 Please don't tell my friends about this problem. It's a ______.
4 The castle has very ______ walls.
5 In the 19th ______ the building was a factory, but it's a hotel now.
6 Toby's parents were at school ______.

A new life in the USA

G past simple: regular verbs
V regular verbs
P regular past simple endings

1 VOCABULARY regular verbs

Write the verbs.

decide ~~invite~~ miss offer pick return visit

1 *invite* friends

2 ______ to go to the USA

3 __________ someone a job

4 __________ fruit

5 __________ a beautiful park

6 __________ your friends and family

7 __________ to your country

2 GRAMMAR past simple: regular verbs

a Complete the sentences with the past simple form of the verb in brackets.

1 We *walked* in the park on Sunday. (walk)

2 They __________ in Hawaii yesterday. (arrive)

3 Lily __________ work early today. (start)

4 The car __________ at the red light. (stop)

5 Cara __________ a lot during the film. (cry)

6 Anne __________ the fish. (like)

b Write negative [–] sentences. Use the words in brackets.

1 Robert talked to Bill. (Tony)
Robert didn't talk to Tony.

2 Clara arrived this morning. (last night)
__________.

3 They opened the door. (the window)
__________.

4 Leo looked at his phone. (his watch)
__________.

5 We travelled by bus. (taxi)
__________.

6 The film started at 8.20. (7.50)
__________.

7 Max cooked fish for dinner. (meat)
__________.

8 Selena booked a ticket to Madrid. (Barcelona)
__________.

c **Re-order the words to make questions.**

1 study where you French did
Where did you study French ______?

2 you school did to yesterday walk
______?

3 in Japan you did when arrive
______?

4 work where last year you did
______?

5 the door did close Joe
______?

6 what study you did yesterday
______?

7 they to talk did the teacher
______?

8 start your class what time did
______?

9 Eva her help with homework you did
______?

10 decide you study did when to economics
______?

d **Write sentences about what you *did* and *didn't* do yesterday. Use the phrases from the list.**

walk to work / school   arrive late at work / school
cook lunch or dinner   help in the house
listen to the radio   phone a friend
play a sport or game   study English   watch TV

I walked to work.
I didn't arrive late at work.
______
______
______
______
______
______
______
______

3 PRONUNCIATION regular past simple endings

a **11.1 Listen and repeat the words. Practise saying the past simple endings.**

 **d**og	 **t**ie	/ɪd/
arriv**ed** listen**ed** travell**ed**	book**ed** stopp**ed** talk**ed**	start**ed** wait**ed** want**ed**

b **Look at the verbs in the list. Circle three past simple endings where -*ed* is pronounced /ɪd/.**

answered asked decided liked looked needed
phoned played rented watched worked

c **11.2 Listen and check. Then listen again and repeat the words.**

4 WORDS AND PHRASES TO LEARN

Complete the sentences with the words from the list.

abroad blueberries public transport
National Park ~~sports club~~ trumpet

1 Helen and Jerry play tennis every weekend at the new sports club.
2 ______ are my favourite fruit.
3 Nasser loves music. He's learning to play the ______.
4 We went travelling in Canada last year. We went walking in the mountains in a beautiful ______.
5 My sister's looking for a job in another country because she wants to live ______.
6 I usually use ______ because I don't have a car.

How was your day?

G past simple irregular verbs: *get*, *go*, *have*, *do*
V verb phrases with *get*, *go*, *have*, *do*
P sentence rhythm

1 VOCABULARY verb phrases with *get*, *go*, *have*, *do*

Complete the sentences with the correct form of *do*, *get*, *go*, or *have*. Use the present simple.

1 They always *get* ___________ up early.

2 She usually ___________ yoga before breakfast.

3 He ___________ a shower at 6.45.

4 They ___________ breakfast in the kitchen.

5 Their children ___________ to school at 8.30.

6 He always ___________ a coffee at 10.30.

7 She ___________ lunch in the office.

8 He ___________ home at 6.00.

9 In the evening, the children ___________ their homework.

10 They usually ___________ dinner at 7.00.

11 The children ___________ to bed at 9.00.

12 They ___________ housework on Saturday morning.

13 She ___________ sport on Saturday afternoon.

14 They sometimes ___________ a nice day out on Sunday.

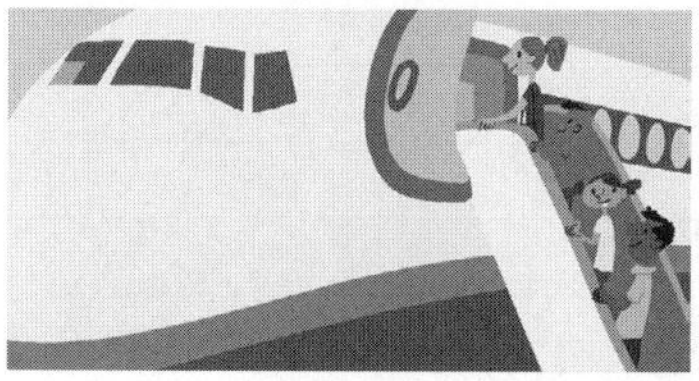

15 In the summer, they ___________ a flight abroad.

16 They ___________ a taxi to the airport.

2 GRAMMAR past simple irregular verbs: *get*, *go*, *have*, *do*

a **Complete the paragraph with the past simple of *get*, *go*, *have* or *do*.**

Yesterday I [1] *got* ___________ up early, I [2] ___________ a coffee, and I [3] ___________ to the gym. After the gym, I [4] ___________ breakfast, and then I [5] ___________ to work. I usually go to work by bus, but yesterday I [6] ___________ a taxi because I was late. For lunch, I [7] ___________ a sandwich with a friend. After work, I [8] ___________ shopping at the supermarket. Then I [9] ___________ home. I [10] ___________ dinner with my family. Then my wife and I [11] ___________ housework. After that, I [12] ___________ to bed early. I was tired!

b Write negative [–] sentences or questions [?].

1 I went to the cinema on Friday. [–]
I didn't go to the cinema on Friday.
2 Isobel had lunch with Tony. [?]
Did Isobel have lunch with Tony?
3 Marisa did housework on Sunday. [–]
____
4 You got up late this morning. [?]
____
5 I had breakfast today. [–]
____
6 Alison got up early yesterday. [–]
____
7 You did your homework last night. [?]
____
8 Peter went to the gym on Tuesday. [?]
____

c Complete the questions and answers.

1 **A** What *did* you *have* for lunch today?
B I ________ a sandwich and a salad.

2 **A** ________ you ________ to the gym after work?
B No, I ________. I ________ dinner with a friend, then I ________ home.

3 **A** ________ Anna ________ the train to work this morning?
B No, she ________. She ________ the bus.

4 **A** ________ Kim ________ her homework?
B Yes, she ________. She ________ her homework on the bus this morning.

5 **A** What ________ you ________ at the weekend?
B Nothing special. I ________ up late, I ________ to the gym, and I ________ shopping.

6 **A** ________ your son ________ up early yesterday?
B No, he ________. He ________ up at 1.00 p.m.!

d Answer the questions about what you did yesterday.

1 What time did you get up?
____
2 Did you have breakfast? What did you have?
____
3 Where did you have lunch? Was it a nice lunch?
____
4 What time did you go home?
____
5 Did you do any homework or housework?
____
6 What did you have for dinner?
____
7 Did you have a good day?
____

3 PRONUNCIATION sentence rhythm

a 11.3 Listen and complete the sentences.

1 Did you *go* ________ to the *gym* ________ *today* ________?
2 ________ did you ________ ________ with?
3 ________ did you ________ ________?
4 Did your friend ________ ________ with you?
5 ________ did you ________ ________?

b Listen again and repeat. Copy the rhythm.

4 WORDS AND PHRASES TO LEARN

Complete the missing words and phrases in the conversations.

1 **A** Hi, darling. H*ow* w*as* y*our* d*ay*?
B Great! I did yoga this morning, then I had lunch with Ava.

2 **A** Did you know Dad a________ Mum t________ m________ him when they were students in Paris?
B Yes, and then they got married there, too!

3 **A** Did you h________ a p________ for your birthday last year?
B Yes, I did. It was fantastic – everyone was there.

4 **A** Hi, Mum. I'm b________!
B Hi, Lucas. Did you have a good day at school?

5 **A** Kiara w________ to h________ for an operation yesterday.
B Oh no... Well, let's visit her tomorrow.

6 Practical English
Is there a bank near here?

asking for and giving directions **V** prepositions of place

1 VOCABULARY prepositions of place

a Complete the words and phrases.

1 *next to*

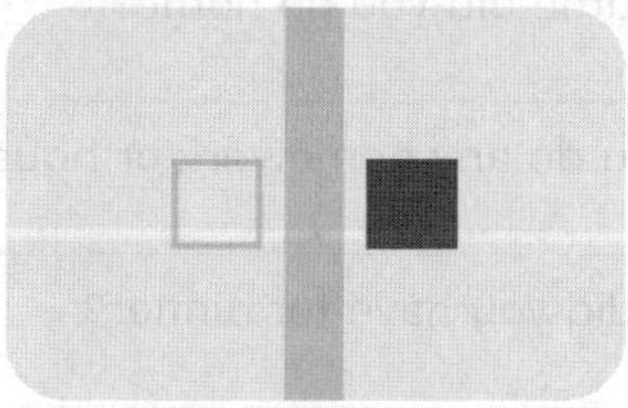

2 __pp__s__t__

3 b__tw____n

4 __n th__ c__rn__r

5 __n th__ l__ft

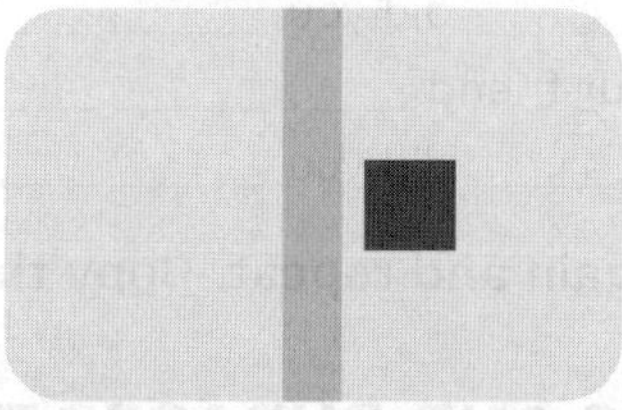

6 __n th__ r__ght

b Look at the map and complete the answers.

1 **A** Where's the park?
B It's *on the corner* of Park Road and East Street.

2 **A** Where's the bank?
B It's ________ the chemist's and the cinema.

3 **A** Where's the hotel?
B It's ________ the bookshop.

4 **A** Where's the cinema?
B It's ________ the bank.

5 **A** Where's the train station?
B It's ________ of East Street and Station Road.

6 **A** Where's the bookshop?
B It's ________ the museum and the Italian restaurant.

7 **A** Where's the hospital?
B It's ________ the chemist's.

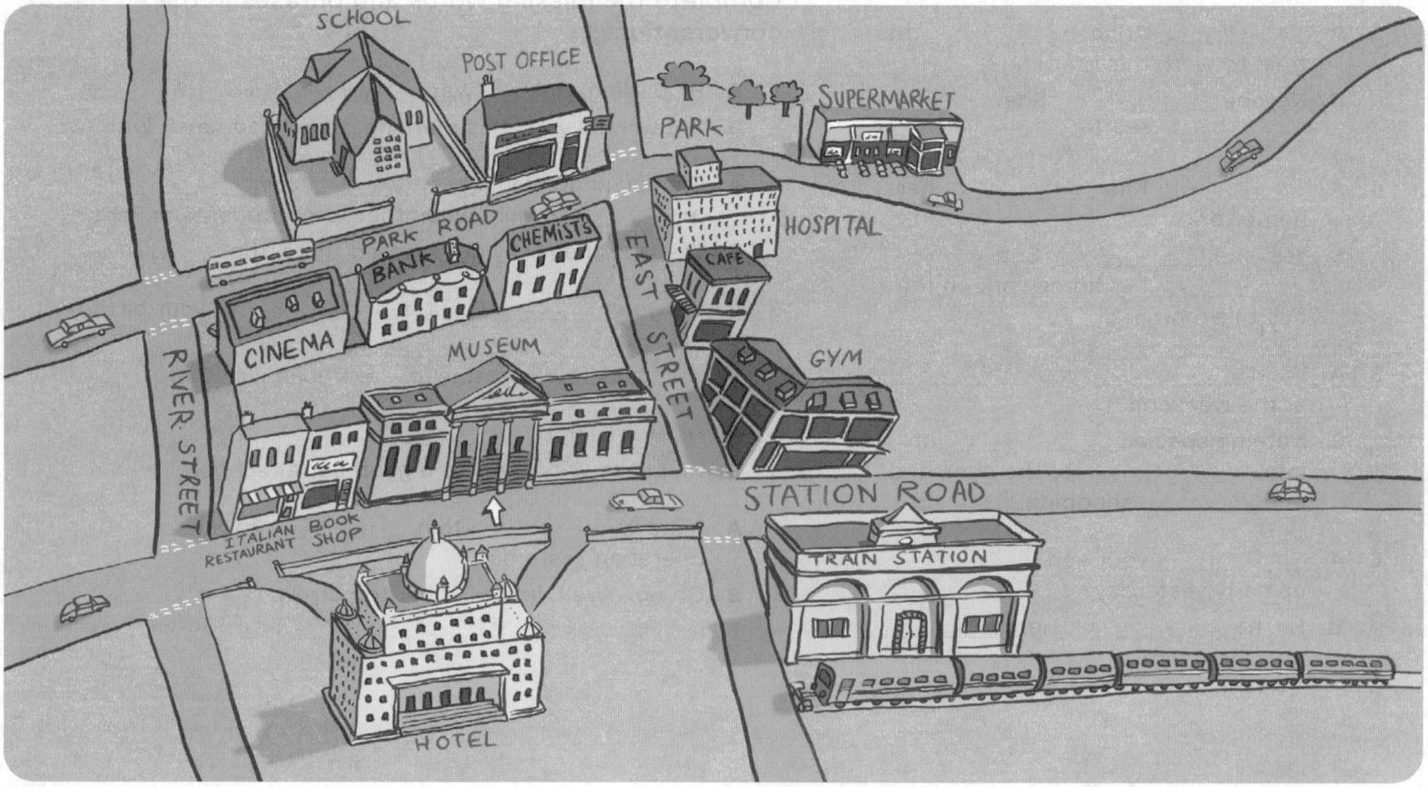

2 ASKING FOR AND GIVING DIRECTIONS

Look at the map again. The people are at the hotel (⇧). Complete the conversations.

1 **A** Excuse me. Where's the *train station*?
B Turn right, go straight on, and it's on the *right*.

2 **A** Excuse me. Where's the post office?
B Turn right, and go straight on, and then turn ________. Go ________ on, and it's on the ________, next to the school.

3 **A** Excuse me. Where's the bank?
B Turn left, and go straight on, and then turn ________. Turn ________ again, and it's on the ________, next to the cinema.

4 **A** Excuse me. Where's the park?
B Turn right, and go straight ________, and then turn ________. Go straight on, and it's on the right, on the ________ of Park Road and East Street.

5 **A** Excuse me. Where's the ________?
B Turn right, go straight on, and it's on the left, opposite the train station.

3 USEFUL PHRASES

Complete the conversations with a phrase from the list.

~~I don't believe it~~ Is there a cash machine near here
It only takes about 15 minutes
this cash machine isn't working Thanks very much
Turn left when you leave the station

1 **A** *I don't believe it*! We're lost again. Excuse me, where's the bookshop?
B Turn left and go straight on. It's next to the coffee shop.

2 **A** Excuse me, ________. Is there another one near here?
B Yes. There's one at the bank opposite the post office.
A Thank you.

3 **A** Excuse me. Where's the museum?
B ________ and go straight on. Then turn right and it's next to the cinema.

4 **A** Excuse me. Where's the station?
B It's in West Street.
A Can I walk there?
B Sure. ________.

5 **A** Excuse me. ________?
B Yes, there's one on the corner of Bridge Street and Station Road, outside the bank.

6 **A** Excuse me. Where's the hospital?
B Turn right and go straight on. Then turn left and it's on the right.
A ________.
B You're welcome.

12A Strangers on a train

G past simple: regular and irregular verbs
V irregular verbs
P irregular verbs

1 VOCABULARY irregular verbs

a Write the past simple form of the verbs.

1 buy *bought*
2 leave ________
3 say ________
4 see ________
5 send ________
6 sit ________
7 tell ________
8 write ________

b Use the words to write positive + or negative – sentences about you.

1 send a message / last night
I sent a message to my sister last night.
2 buy new clothes / last month
I didn't buy new clothes last month.
3 see my friends / last weekend
____
4 leave the house early / this morning
____
5 sit next to a friend / in the last class
____
6 write an email / yesterday
____
7 tell a story to a child / last night
____
8 say hello to a stranger / last week
____

2 PRONUNCIATION irregular verbs

a Write the past simple verbs in the chart.

~~bought~~ left said saw sent told

 1 horse	 2 ph**o**ne	 3 **e**gg
bought		

b 12.1 **Listen and check. Listen again and repeat the words.**

3 GRAMMAR past simple: regular and irregular verbs

a Write the past simple forms of the verbs.

1 arrive *arrived*
2 ask ________
3 do ________
4 get up ________
5 go ________
6 have ________
7 rent ________
8 stay ________
9 visit ________
10 wait ________

b Complete the sentences with the past simple form of a verb from a.

1 I *went* to Türkiye for my holidays last year.
2 I ________ very late this morning.
3 We ________ at the airport at six o'clock in the evening.
4 I ________ dinner in a restaurant last night.
5 I ________ for the bus for two hours.
6 We ________ in a hotel near the beach.
7 I ________ my girlfriend to marry me in Rome.
8 I ________ a lot of exercise last week.
9 My parents ________ us last weekend.
10 I ________ a bike to travel round the island.

c **Use the words to write past simple sentences and questions.**

1 where / you / get married
*Where did you get married*________________?
2 I / not like / the food in that restaurant
________________.
3 we / see / a good film last night
________________.
4 you / not call / me yesterday
________________.
5 why / you buy / a new car
________________?
6 they / book / the tickets online
________________.
7 he / send / me a text this morning
________________.
8 you / go to work / by train yesterday
________________?
9 she / not want / a coffee
________________.
10 you / tell / me your address
________________?

d **Complete the conversation with the past simple form of the verbs in brackets.**

A Jack! Over here!
B Pippa! It's great to see you!
A [1] *Did you have* ________ a good trip? (you / have)
B Yes, thanks. [2] ________ fine. (it / be)
A Are you hungry?
B No, [3] ________ lunch on the train. (I / have)
A Really? What [4] ________? (you / have)
B Some sandwiches. [5] ________ them at the station this morning. (I / buy)
A Good idea. [6] ________ to the station? (you / drive)
B No, [7] ________ a taxi. (I / get)
A Did you? What time [8] ________ home? (you / leave)
B [9] ________ at seven o'clock. (the taxi / arrive)
A That's early! Are you tired?
B A bit. [10] ________ well last night. (I / not sleep)
A Well, here's my car. Let's go home and you can relax.

4 WORDS AND PHRASES TO LEARN

Complete the missing words and phrases in the conversations.

1 **A** Did you have a good journey?
B No, I didn't sit down for two hours because the train was f*ull*________.

2 **A** My grandparents went to China last year.
B Th________ i________! Where did they go?

3 **A** Can you buy the t________ for the concert today?
B Yes, I can go to the box office after work. What day would you like to go?

4 **A** What time is it? Is it t________ to g________?
B Yes, it is. It's 9.45 and the class starts at 10.00.

5 **A** Did you ex________ numbers with the girl you met at the party?
B Yes, but she didn't call me.

6 **A** Mmm, that's a n________ s________. Is Dad cooking?
B Yes, he's making a chocolate cake.

12B Revise the past

G past simple revision
V revision of past verb forms
P past simple, sentence rhythm

1 VOCABULARY revision of past verb forms

a Match 1–8 to a–h.

1 My parents stayed _e_   a to go home.
2 I booked ___   b our flights on my phone.
3 We packed ___   c my family when I was in the USA.
4 I missed ___   d our suitcases last night.
5 She sent ___   e ~~in a hotel near the beach.~~
6 We rented ___   f a car at the airport.
7 I waited ___   g for the bus for half an hour.
8 We didn't want ___   h me four messages yesterday.

b Complete the sentences with the correct form of *do*, *go*, *have* or *get*.

1 Did you _have_ a nice day yesterday?
2 Max was tired so he ___ to bed early last night.
3 Did you ___ yoga yesterday?
4 It was a beautiful day, so we ___ lunch in the garden.
5 Sorry I'm late. I ___ the bus this morning and the traffic was terrible.
6 I ___ to Italy for my summer holiday. It was amazing.
7 Anya ___ a lot of sport when she was at school.
8 We ___ a taxi from the airport. It was really expensive.
9 I ___ a shower after breakfast.
10 Duncan ___ his homework at the weekend.
11 John and Dina ___ married in the summer.
12 We ___ to an exhibition at the National Gallery.

2 GRAMMAR past simple revision

a Complete the sentences with the [+] or [–] past simple form of a verb from the list.

~~buy~~ leave ~~say~~ see tell write

1 [+] I _bought_ some new jeans on Saturday.
2 [–] He _didn't say_ goodbye after the party.
3 [+] I ___ the answer on a piece of paper.
4 Were you at work yesterday? [–] I ___ you.
5 [+] We ___ the police officer our names and addresses.
6 [–] I ___ the house yesterday.

b Complete the conversations.

1 **A** _Where_ _were_ _you_ last night?
B I was at the cinema.

2 **A** ___ ___ ___ ___ last night?
B No, I stayed at home.

3 **A** ___ ___ at school this morning?
B Yes, I was.

4 **A** ___ ___ ___ ___ ___ ___ ___ last night?
B I went to bed at 10.30.

5 **A** ___ ___ ___ ___ to the shops?
B Because I needed to buy some bread.

6 **A** ___ ___ ___ ___ for breakfast this morning?
B Just toast and coffee.

c **Complete the text with the past simple form of the verbs in the list.**

be get (x2) ~~go~~ have (x3) listen make sit watch

Last Sunday, we [1] *got* ______ up early and [2] *went* ______ to the river. We walked for about an hour and then we [3] ______ a coffee outside a small café. We [4] ______ home at about 1.00 and then I [5] ______ lunch for the family. We [6] ______ vegetable soup, and then chicken and pasta. The weather [7] ______ nice, so after lunch I [8] ______ on a comfortable chair in the garden and [9] ______ to music and relaxed. In the evening, we [10] ______ a pizza for dinner and then we [11] ______ a film together. A perfect slow Sunday!

d **What did you do last Sunday? Write five sentences.**

1 ______
2 ______
3 ______
4 ______
5 ______

3 PRONUNCIATION past simple, sentence rhythm

a **12.2 Listen and (circle) the word with a different sound.**

/ɪd/	1 invit**ed** (pack**ed**) rent**ed**
/d/ dog	2 arriv**ed** play**ed** decid**ed**
/ɒ/ clock	3 s**a**t w**a**s w**a**nted
/eɪ/ train	4 r**ai**ned pl**ay**ed s**ai**d
/ɔː/ horse	5 b**ough**t wr**o**te s**aw**

b **Listen again and repeat the words.**

c **12.3 Listen and complete the questions.**

1 *Did* ______ you *go* ______ *to* ______ school today?

2 ______ you ______ a good day?

3 ______ ______ ______ ______ holiday?

4 ______ the last film ______?

5 ______ ______ you did sport?

6 ______ ______ ______ this morning?

d **Listen again and repeat the questions. Copy the rhythm.**

OXFORD
UNIVERSITY PRESS

Great Clarendon Street, Oxford, OX2 6DP, United Kingdom

Oxford University Press is a department of the University of Oxford. It furthers the University's objective of excellence in research, scholarship, and education by publishing worldwide. Oxford is a registered trade mark of Oxford University Press in the UK and in certain other countries

First published in 2025
2029 2028 2027 2026 2025
10 9 8 7 6 5 4 3 2 1

ISBN: 978 0 19 414917 4

Printed in China

This book is printed on paper from certified and well-managed sources

ACKNOWLEDGEMENTS

The authors would like to thank all the teachers and students round the world whose feedback has helped us to shape English File.

The authors would also like to thank: all those at Oxford University Press (both in Oxford and around the world) and the design team who have contributed their skills and ideas to producing this course.

Finally very special thanks from Clive to Maria Angeles, Lucia, and Eric, and from Christina to Cristina, for all their support and encouragement. Christina would also like to thank her children Joaquin, Marco, and Krysia for their constant inspiration.

The publisher would like to thank the following for their permission to reproduce photographs: Alamy (Jan Tadeusz, Golden Pixels LLC, grzegorz knec, Ingram Publishing, ANDREW WALTERS, Studioshots, Tades Yee, Ben Molyneux Spanish collection, Julio Bulnes, LJSphotography, Hero Images Inc., Robert Convery, Kumar Sriskandan, Image Farm Inc., iPhone, neil guegan, Image Source, Cultura Creative, Takatoshi Kurikawa, Beyond Fotomedia GmbH, PhotoAlto; Getty Images (MStudioImages, Mixmike, andresr, Ugurhan Betin, Peter Dazeley, Leland Bobbe, Blend Images/Hill Street Studios; Oxford University Press (Masterfile/Robert Harding, Mark Mason, C Squared Studios, Wilhelmus Pictor, Gareth Boden, Superstock/Photononstop, iStock/Spiderstock, Mike Stone, Martin Hospach, Richard Ponsford, Photodisc, iStock/pearleye, Image Source; Shutterstock (rui vale sousa, Zhao jian kang, kavalenkau, Vincent St. Thomas, cornfield, Tayvay, aminphotoz, Dmytro Larin, BestStockFoto, Takayuki, Andrea Raffin, azure1, Zigres, Jack Jelly, Choi jae young, feeling lucky, Sergey Peterman, Kaspars Grinvalds, erzetic, Rusly95, photo25th, Peter Kotoff, Antonio Guillem, Kinga, fizkes, OKcamera, Stanislav Boxer, New Africa, Nemanja Zotovic, Lipowski Milan, Kotomiti Okuma, tavi, Photoongraphy, Sarawut Aiemsinsuk, billy bonns, Billion Photos, Vitaly Korovin, 24Novembers, design56, ILYA AKINSHIN, VH-studio, Dario Sabljak, Pixfiction, alicja neumiler, Seregam, Jesus Cervantes, windu, Yury Gulakov, Surrphoto, ESB Professional, NY-P, Chones, jooh, Africa Studio, Bozhena Melnyk, Tim UR, Photographee, Artem and Olga Sapegin, Oliver Hoffmann, Gayvoronskaya Yana, mimagephotography, WAYHOME studio, T.TATSU, El Nariz, CebotariN, Prostock-studio, Kenneth Man, Charles T. Bennett, michaeljung, Monkey Business Images, Kzenon, GaudiLab, StockLite, Robert Kneschke, Gorodenkoff, Jacob Lund, wavebreakmedia, Daniel Krason, antpkr, Tish1, Claudio Divizia, NT_Studio, AnnaStills, Popova Valeriya, sanneberg, Evgeny Litvinov, medvedsky, Selin Aydogan, BearFotos, franz12, AboutLife, Ruslan Guzov, Matthew Dixon, S.Borisov); Shutterstock Editorial (Paramount/Kobal, Warner Bros/Kobal/REX, Moviestore, Danjaq/EON Productions/Kobal, Regency Enterprises/Kobal, Paramount Pictures/Bad Robot/Kobal, Columbia/The Weinstein Company/Kobal, Warner Bros./Courtesy Everett Collection, Dreamworks Animation/Kobal).

Illustrations by: Mark Duffin; Atushi Hara/Dutch Uncle; John Haslam; Adam Larkum/Illustration Ltd.; Sean Longcroft; Roger Penwill.
Pronunciation chart artwork by: Ellis Nadler.

The manufacturer's authorised representative in the EU for product safety is
Oxford University Press España S.A. of el Parque Empresarial San Fernando de Henares, Avenida de Castilla, 2 – 28830 Madrid (www.oup.es/en)

Leckie × Leckie
Scotland's leading educational publishers

CW01655574

Practice Papers for SQA Exams

Higher

Human Biology

01/300310

ISBN 978-1-84372-797-2

Published by
Leckie & Leckie Ltd, 4 Queen Street, Edinburgh, EH2 1JE
Tel: 0131 220 6831 Fax: 0131 225 9987
enquiries@leckieandleckie.co.uk www.leckieandleckie.co.uk

A CIP Catalogue record for this book is available from the British Library.

Questions and answers in this book do not emanate from SQA. All of our entirely new and original Practice Papers have been written by experienced authors working directly for the publisher.

This book is dedicated to Ronald Gaffin, a great friend and wonderful Bridge partner.

Introduction

Layout of the book

The papers which follow have been produced to give you practice in two of the elements needed for Outcomes 1 and 2 of Higher Human Biology. The first element is "Knowledge and Understanding" [KU] which depends on you being familiar with all the theory, especially important in Human Biology which is very much a knowledge-based subject. You need to know the facts, concepts and common techniques. The second element is "Problem Solving" [PS] which tests your ability to select relevant information from a variety of sources, present information in a variety of forms, process information, plan, design and evaluate the design of experiments, draw valid conclusions and give explanations, and make predictions and generalisations. These two elements, which are assessed by the National Examination, are combined to produce your overall grade. As a very rough guide, you will be awarded a pass at A, B or C if you obtain around 75%, 65% or 55% respectively.

You are also required to produce an internal report of an experiment which will be assessed by your teacher. This report is evidence that Outcome 3 (collect and analyse information related to Higher Human Biology obtained by experiment) for the Higher Human Biology has been satisfied. No marks are allocated to this in the National Examination.

All three papers have been modelled on actual National Examinations. The layout, colour and question level of all three papers are very similar to the actual exam that you will sit, so that you can become familiar with what the exam paper will look like. In addition, the format of the questions reflects what you are likely to encounter in the National Examination. All parts of the syllabus have been represented in these papers.

Each paper has three sections, A, B and C.

Section A consists of 30 multiple-choice questions, of which approximately 20 test Knowledge and Understanding and the remaining 10 or 50 test Problem Solving. This section is worth 30 marks and is answered on a separate grid.

Section B consists of short-answer questions which contain mixture of knowledge and understanding and problem-solving questions in a ratio of 3:2 as explained above. This section is worth 80 marks. These questions are answered on the paper itself.

Section C consists of two extended responses, both of which test knowledge and understanding. The first is structured, being in parts with marks allocated to each part shown. You will choose one question from two here. The second is unstructured, again with a choice of one from two. This section is worth 20 marks. These are answered on the blank pages provided in the examination booklet.

In the unstructured questions, two marks are allocated for coherence and relevance.

Coherence really means how well the essay hangs together, flows from one point, or paragraph, logically to the next. An obvious way to achieve this is to divide your answer up into paragraphs which deal with the question in logical chunks. For example, a question such as "*Discuss the role of enzymes as catalysts*" could be answered under subheadings such as "*Catalysts*", "*Properties*", "*Specificity*" and so forth. Dividing up your answer in this way helps ensure the flow of ideas and makes it more likely that you will be awarded the mark. Sometimes you can take the subheadings from the actual question. For example "*Give an account of the role of the pituitary gland in controlling normal growth and development and describe the effects of named drugs on fetal development.*" This could be answered under the headings "*Role of the pituitary*" and "*Effects of named drugs on fetal development.*" It is very important that related material should be kept together. In general, you need to aim to have at least five correct points to be able to get the mark for coherence.

Relevance is a major problem for many candidates. In general, an answer should cover at least ten relevant points. The inclusion of irrelevant information, even if it is correct information, will gain you no marks. If, for example, you are asked a question about aerobic respiration and you give information about anaerobic respiration, even if it is correct, this will deemed irrelevant. In other words, stick to the question and try not to deviate from it. Again, you need to aim for at least five correct points to be able to get the mark for relevance.

The answer section is at the back of this book. Each answer contains, where appropriate, some guidance as to how it was obtained, practical tips on how to tackle certain types of questions, details of how marks are awarded and advice on just what the examiners will be looking for. Also included is the type of question it is: Knowledge and Understanding [KU] or Problem Solving [PS].

How to use this book

Interacting with learning material is a powerful means of obtaining feedback on your strengths and weaknesses. The material in this book will give you an excellent way of working on different strategies needed to handle the actual National Examination. Seeking help, where needed, from your teacher is vital to improvement and building up your confidence and expertise.

The practice papers can be used in two main ways:

1. You can complete an entire practice paper as preparation for the final exam. If you would like to use the book in this way, you can either complete the practice paper under exam style conditions by setting yourself a time for each paper and answering it as well as possible without using any references or notes. Alternatively, you can answer the practice paper questions as a revision exercise, using your notes to produce a model answer. Your teacher may mark these for you.
2. You can use the Topic Index at the front of this book to find all the questions within the book that deal with a specific topic in any of the three Units. This allows you to focus specifically on areas that you particularly want to revise or, if you are mid way through your course, it lets you practise answering exam-style questions for just those topics that you have studied. You will find this useful if you want to practice handling particular types of problem solving questions.

Revision advice

The need to work out a plan for regular and methodical revision is obvious. If you leave things to the last minute, it may result in panic and stress which will stop you from performing at your best. If you need help, it is best to find this out when there is time to get help. Revision planners are highly individual so you need to produce one which suits you. Use an area of your home which is set aside only for studying if possible so that you form a positive link between this place and doing nothing but revision and studying. In this way you will be less liable to distractions. Not only do you need a plan for revising Higher Human Biology, but also for all your subjects. Below is one version but you will have your own ideas here!

Work out a revision timetable for each week's work in advance – remember to cover all of your subjects and to leave time for homework and breaks. For example:

Day	*6pm–6.45pm*	*7pm–8pm*	*8.15pm–9pm*	*9.15pm–10pm*
Monday	Homework	Homework	English revision	Human Biology revision
Tuesday	Maths revision	Physics revision	Homework	Free
Wednesday	Geography revision	Modern Studies revision	English revision	French revision
Thursday	Homework	Maths revision	Human Biology revision	Free
Friday	Geography revision	French revision	Free	Free
Saturday	Free	Free	Free	Free
Sunday	Modern Studies revision	Maths revision	Modern Studies revision	Homework

Make sure that you have at least one evening free a week to relax, socialise and recharge your batteries. It also gives your brain a chance to process the information that you have been feeding it all week.

Arrange your study time into sessions which suit you, with a break in between e.g. 6pm–6.45pm, 7pm–8pm, 8.15pm–9pm, 9.15pm–10pm. Try to begin to studying as early as possible in the evening when your brain is still alert and be aware that the longer you delay, the harder it will be to start.

If you miss a session, don't panic. Log this and make it up as soon as possible. Don't get behind in your schedule. Discipline is everything in being a successful student.

Study a different subject in each session, except for the day before an exam.

Do something different during the breaks between study sessions – have a cup of tea, or listen to some music. Don't let your 15 minutes expand into 20 or 25 minutes!

Have your class notes and any textbooks available for your revision to hand as well as plenty of blank paper, a pen, etc. You may like to make keyword sheets like the example below:

Keyword	*Meaning*
Synapse	Gap between nerve cells
Corpus callosum	Structure in brain connecting two halves of the cerebrum

Flash cards are an excellent way of practising terms and definitions. You can make these easily or buy them very cheaply. Use flash cards either to recall the keyword when you see the meaning or to give the meaning when you see the keyword.

Finally, forget or ignore all or some of the advice in this section if you are happy with your present way of studying. Everyone revises differently, so find a way that works for you!

Command words

In the practice papers and in the National Examination itself, a number of "command words" will be used in the questions. These command words are used to show you how you should answer a question – some words indicate that you should write more than others. If you familiarise yourself with these command words, it will help you to structure your answers more effectively.

Command word	*Meaning/explanation*
Name, state, identify, list	Giving a list is acceptable here – as a general rule you will get one mark for each point you give.
Suggest	Give more than a list – perhaps a proposal or an idea.
Outline	Give a brief description or overview of what you are talking about.
Describe	Give more detail than you would in an outline, and use examples where you can.
Explain	Discuss why an action has been taken or an outcome reached – what are the reasons and/or processes behind it?
Justify	Give reasons for your answer, stating why you have taken an action or reached a particular conclusion.
Define	Give the meaning of the term.
Compare/contrast	Give the key features of 2 different items or ideas and discuss their similarities/differences.
Predict	Work out what will happen.

In the Examination

Watch your time and pace yourself carefully. Work out roughly how much time you can spend on each answer and try to stick to this.

Be clear before the examination what the instructions are likely to be, e.g. how many questions you should answer in each section. The practice papers will help you to become familiar with the examination instructions.

Read the question thoroughly before you begin to answer it – make sure you know exactly what the question is asking you to do. If the question is in sections, e.g. 15(*a*), 15(*b*), 15(*c*), make sure that you can answer each section before you start writing.

Plan your extended responses by jotting down keywords, by making a brief mind map of the important points or by doing whatever you find works best for you. Don't repeat yourself because you will not get any more marks for saying the same thing twice. This also applies to annotated diagrams which will not get you any extra marks if the information is repeated in the written part of your answer.

Give proper explanations. A common error is to give descriptions rather than explanations. If you are asked to explain something, you should be giving reasons. Check your answer to an 'explain' question and make sure that you have used linking words and phrases such as 'because', 'this means that', 'therefore', 'so', 'so that', 'due to', 'since' and 'the reason is'.

Good luck!

Topic Index

Unit	*Topic*	*Exam 1*	*Exam 2*	*Exam 3*
1. CELL FUNCTION AND INHERITANCE	The role of enzymes in cell metabolism	A2	B1(a)–(e), C2A	B3
	Protein synthesis	B1(a), (b) B2(c)	A1, A2, A30	A6, A7, B1(a), (b), (c)
	Energy transfer	A3, C1A	A4, B4	A1, A2, A14, C2B
	Cell transport	B1(a), B9(d)	A3 B1 (d) (i)	C2A
	Cellular response in defence	A4, C1B	A12, A14 B2(a)–(c)	A30, B1(c)
	Inheritance	A9 A17, B4(c), B5(a), (b), B8(a), (e)	B9(a), (b)	A3, A4, A8, A21, B4(b), (c), (d)
2. THE CONTINUATION OF LIFE	Reproduction	A7, B5(c), B6	A8, C1A	A10, A11, A28, B5(a), (b)
	Development	A8	B7	A29, B5(c)
	Transport mechanisms	B1(c), B7, B9(a), (e)	A10, A15, C2B	B6
	Delivery of materials to cells	B9(b), (c)	A9 B1(d) (ii)	A15, B8(ii), C1B
	Removal of materials from blood	B9(b)	A22 B1(f)	A20, B8 (a), (b) (i)
	Regulating mechanisms	A15, C1A	A11, B10	A22, B9
3. BEHAVIOUR, POPULATIONS AND ENVIRONMENT	Nervous system and memory	A11, A12, A14, A20 B11(a), (b), (c), (d), 12(a)	A28, A29, B12, C1B	A26, B11
	Behaviour	A22, A23	A23, A24, A27, B11	A27, C1A
	Population growth and development	A18, A19, A27, A28, A29, A30, B13, C1B	A18, A19	A23

Unit	*Topic*	*Exam 1*	*Exam 2*	*Exam 3*
4. PROBLEM SOLVING SKILLS	• Select relevant information	A6, A21, B8(b), (c), (d)(i), B10(a)	A5, A16, A17, A20 B5(a), B6(a), (d)	A25, B2(a), B4(a), B7(a) (ii) (iii) (iv)
	• Present information appropriately	B3(b)	B3 (a), B13(a)	B12(b)
	• Process information accurately	A1, A5, A10, A13, A16 B2(a), (b), (d) B3(a), B4(a), B10(b), (d), B11(e)	A7, A13, A25, A26 B3(b), B5(b), (c), B6(b), (c) B9 (c), B13(d)	A5, A12, A13, A16, 7(b), B12(a)
	• Plan, design and evaluate experimental procedures	A26, B3(c), B10(e)	B6(f), (g) B8(b), (c), (d), B13(c)	B2(c), B10(b), B12(d), (e)
	• Draw valid conclusions and give explanations	A25, B(d)(ii), B10(c)	B3(c), B5(a), B8(a), B13(b)	A18, A19, B2(d), B4(a), 7(a) (i), B10(a), B12(c)
	• Make predictions and generalisations	A24, B10(f), B12(b)	A6, A21, B6(e)	A9, A17, A24, B2(b)

Exam 1

Leckie × Leckie
Scotland's leading educational publishers

Answer sheet for Section A:

Higher Human Biology
Practice Papers for SQA Exams

Please select your answer using a single mark e.g. A B C D

	A	B	C	D
1.				
2.				
3.				
4.				
5.				
6.				
7.				
8.				
9.				
10.				
11.				
12.				
13.				
14.				
15.				

	A	B	C	D
16.				
17.				
18.				
19.				
20.				
21.				
22.				
23.				
24.				
25.				
26.				
27.				
28.				
29.				
30.				

Higher Human Biology

Practice Papers for SQA Exams

Time allowed: 1 hour 45 minutes

Exam 1

Fill in these boxes and read what is printed below.

Full name of school

Town

Forename(s)

Surname

Read each question carefully.

Attempt **all** questions.

Write your answers on the blank paper provided.

Write as neatly as possible.

Answer in sentences wherever possible.

Leckie × Leckie
Scotland's leading educational publishers

Read closely

1. For Section A, you should use an HB pencil and, where neccesary, a rubber.
2. Each Answer is **either** A, B, C or D. When you have decided your answer, use your pencil to put a line in the appropriate space on the answer sheet. (See the example below.)
3. Each question has **only one correct** answer.
4. Do not do any rough working on the answer sheet: use a separate sheet of paper.

Sample question

The surface area:volume ratio of a cube with edges 1 cm is

A 1:1

B 3:1

C **6**:1

D 12:1

The correct answer is **C** – 6:1. This answer has been clearly marked in **pencil** below.

Changing an answer

If you need to change an answer, carefully rub out your original, then use your pencil to fill in the answer you now want. Below, the answer has been changed to **D**.

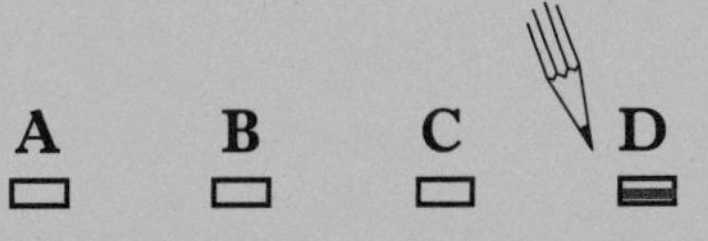

SECTION A

All questions in this section should be attempted.
Answers should be given on the separate answer sheet provided.

1. Part of a DNA molecule contains 250 bases. Of these bases, 60 are cytosine.

The percentage of thymine bases present in this part of the DNA is

A 12%

B 13%

C 24%

D 26%

2. Which of the following statements is **true**?

A Enteropeptidase activates trypsin.

B Vitamins generally do not act as co-enzymes.

C A co-factor is a protein substance.

D Enzyme specificity depends on the structure of the active site.

3. Which of the following is **not** a function of lipids? They act as

A an immediate energy source

B insulators of nerve fibres

C transporters of vitamins

D shock absorbers on hands and feet.

4. The swine flu virus is made up almost entirely of

A protein and ribonucleic acid

B ribonucleic acid and lipid

C carbohydrate and lipid

D carbohydrate and ribonucleic acid.

5. A technician needs to make up 200 cm^3 of 0·9% salt solution from a 1·8% stock solution.

She can do this by

A adding 100 cm^3 of water to 100 cm^3 of the stock solution

B adding 50 cm^3 of water to 150 cm^3 of the stock solution

C diluting the stock solution ten times

D concentrating the stock solution ten times.

6. The key shown below is used to identify unknown carbohydrates.

1 Soluble 2
Insoluble ....Starch
2 Clinistix test positive....Glucose
Clinistix test negative ...3
3 Barfoed's test positive...Fructose
Barfoed's test negative ... Lactose

Which of the following statements is **not** true?

A Lactose is soluble and does not react with Clinistix.

B Fructose is insoluble and reacts with Barfoed's.

C Glucose is soluble and reacts with Clinistix.

D Only one of the four carbohydrates is insoluble.

7. Which of the following is **not** true?

A Oxytocin is produced by the pituitary.

B Progesterone is a placental hormone.

C Oestrogen is produced by the ovaries.

D Follicle stimulating hormone inhibits oestrogen.

8. Dizygotic twins result from

A a single ovum being fertilised by a single sperm

B a single ovum being fertilised by two different sperm

C two ova being fertilised by one sperm

D two ova being fertilised by two different sperm.

9. During the first meiotic division, which of the following are separated?

A Chromatids

B Chromosomes

C Centromeres

D Chiasmata

10. The table below shows some results of measurements made on taken from a girl before and immediately after exercise.

	Breaths per minute	*Volume of each breath (cm^3)*	*% oxygen in air breathed out*
Before exercise	15	300	18
After exercise	30	1200	15

The girl's breathing rate did not change for about fifteen minutes after the exercise. During the first five minutes after exercise, what would be the total volume of oxygen breathed out?

A 27 litres

B 2·7 litres

C 2700 cm^3

D 270 cm^3

11. The diagram below shows the human brain. Which of the structures controls conscious thought?

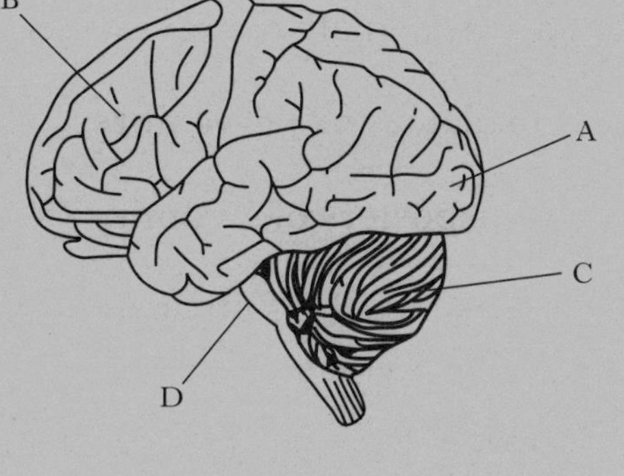

12. The diagram below shows a simple human reflex arc.

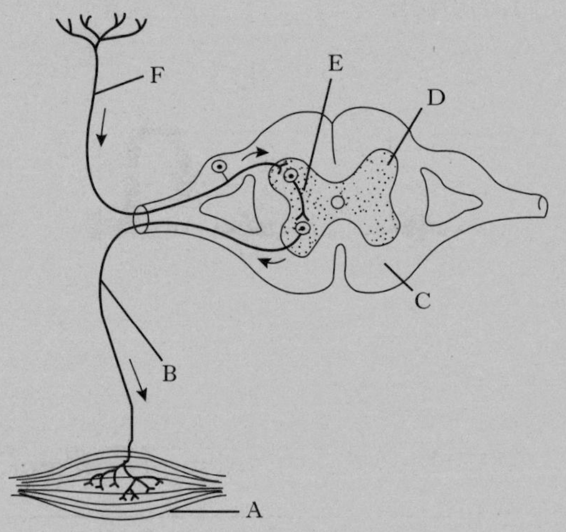

Which of the following statements is **true**?

A B is a motor neurone and A is a receptor.

B F is a sensory neurone and C is grey matter.

C E is a relay neurone and D is grey matter.

D A is an effector and D is white matter.

13. The graph below shows the trace of a human heart beat.

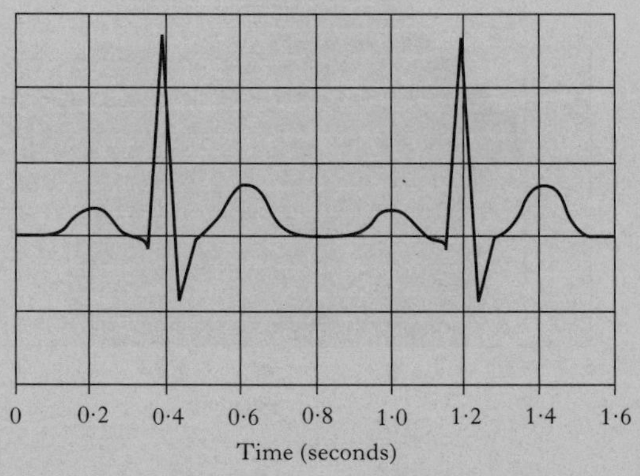

How many beats per minute is the heart rate?

A 65

B 70

C 75

D 80

14. Which of the following shows the correct effect of the autonomic nervous system?

	Body structure	*Effect*	*Branch of autonomic nervous system*
A	heart	rate of beat increases	parasympathetic
B	smooth muscle in bronchioles	muscles become relaxed	parasympathetic
C	stomach	muscle wall contractions increase	sympathetic
D	sweat gland	activity increases	sympathetic

15. Which of the following causes a reduction in the blood glucose levels?

A Antidiuretic hormone

B Adrenalin

C Insulin

D Glucagon

16. Two students, John and James, were given some fruit juice to drink and the change in their respective blood glucose levels was checked every 30 minutes. The results are shown in the table below.

Time after drinking juice (minutes)	*Blood glucose level ($mg/100\ cm^3$)*	
	John	*James*
0	85	87
30	140	165
60	90	100
90	85	90

Which of the following statements is **correct**?

A After 30 minutes, John's blood glucose level was twice his original.

B James's blood glucose level dropped by approximately 40% between 30 and 60 minutes after drinking the juice.

C After 60 minutes, James's blood glucose concentration was approximately 20% greater than John's.

D John took longer than James to return to his original blood sugar level.

17. A man who is colour-blind, a sex-linked recessive condition, marries a woman who is not a carrier for this condition and is completely free from any symptoms of the condition. They have one daughter who is colour-blind and one son who is unaffected. In the table below the symbols B and b are used for the normal and affected alleles respectively.

Which line gives the genotypes of the son and daughter?

	Son	*Daughter*
A	X^bY	X^BX^B
B	X^BY	X^BX^b
C	X^bY	X^BX^b
D	X^BY	X^bX^b

18. Which of the following would be used to calculate the overall change in the size of a population?

A Adding births to deaths and then subtracting both emigrations and immigrations.

B Adding births to emigrations and then subtracting both deaths and immigrations.

C Adding deaths to emigrations and then subtracting both births and immigrations.

D Adding births to immigrations and then subtracting both deaths and emigrations.

19. Which of the following processes would tend to decrease atmospheric carbon dioxide?

A Respiration

B Nitrogen fixation

C Photosynthesis

D Decomposition

20. The diagram below represents a model of how memory might function.

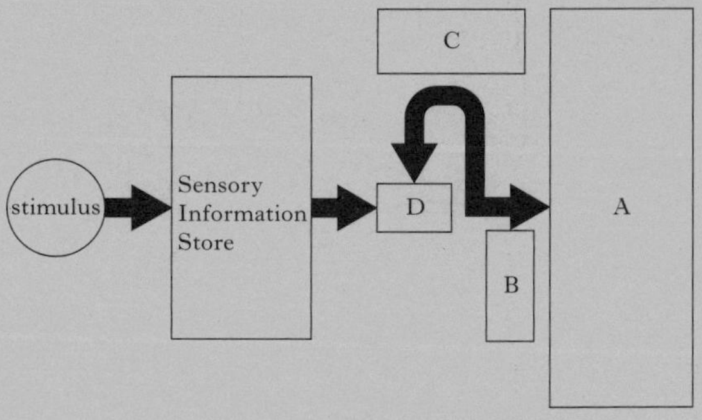

Which of the following is correct?

	Name	*Function*
A	short-term memory	holds unlimited amount of information
B	long-term memory	holds limited amount of information
C	rehearsal	helps transfer information from short to long-term memory
D	elaboration	helps transfer information from long to short-term memory

21. A population pyramid for a state in America in 2000 is shown below.

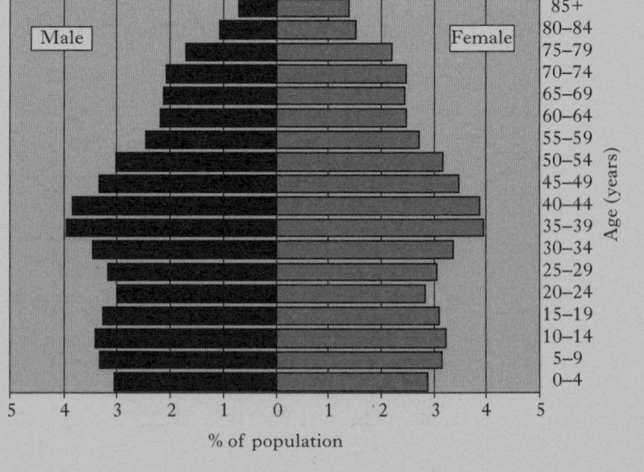

Approximately what percentage of males are between the ages of 50 and 59 years of age?

A 4·5

B 5·5

C 6·5

D 7·5

22. A boy was bitten by a snake. Afterwards he was afraid of all snakes. This is an example of

A deindividuation

B social facilitation

C generalisation

D discrimination.

23. In studying the relative importance of inheritance versus environmental influences, a good choice of human subjects would be

A monozygotic twins raised in very similar environments

B monozygotic twins raised in very different environments

C dizygotic twins raised in very similar environments

D dizygotic twins raised in very different environments.

24. The following diagram shows part of a metabolic pathway and the genes (G1 and G2) which are responsible for producing the specific enzymes (E1 and E2) to catalyse the conversion of one metabolite into the next one.

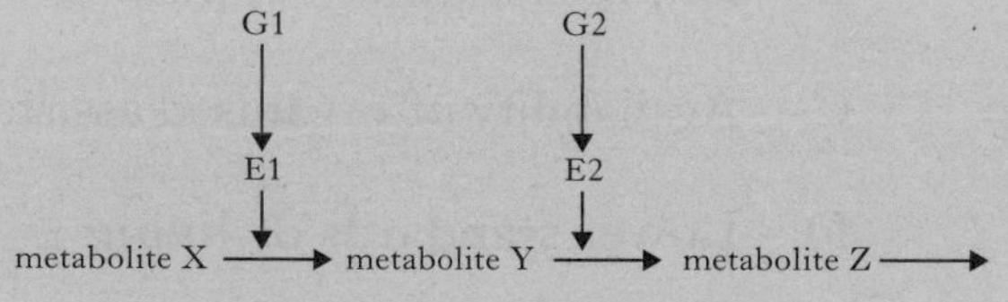

If a mutation occurred which prevented one of these genes from functioning properly, which of the following would happen?

A G1 mutation would cause X to accumulate.

B G1 mutation would cause Y to accumulate.

C G2 mutation would cause E2 to accumulate.

D G2 mutation would cause Z to accumulate.

25. The graph below shows the effect of repetition (number of practice trials) on the time taken to perform a particular task.

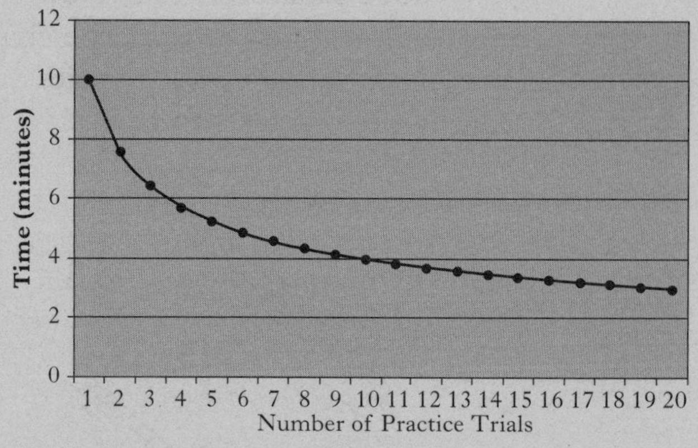

Which of the following is a reasonable conclusion from this data?

A The improvement in performance was uniform over the trial period

B Practising this particular task does not improve performance

C Improvement was most evident in the early trials

D Continued trials would reduce the time taken to almost zero

26. The following diagram shows a simple demonstration of the effect of ATP on dead muscle tissue. Two different solutions, ATP and glucose, were added separately to two different muscle strands as shown. The change in length after 20 minutes was recorded for each strand.

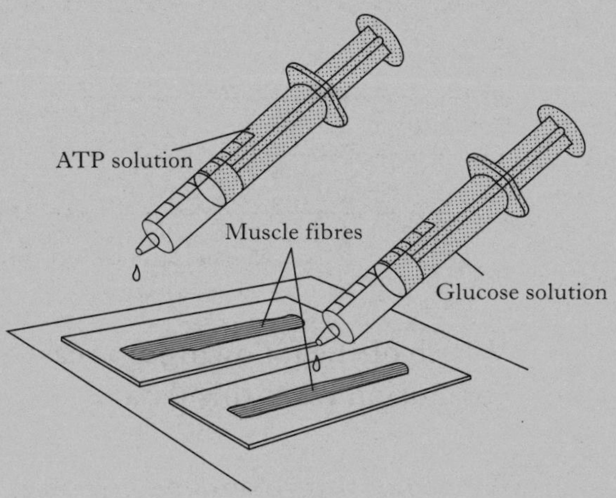

Which of the following would **not** improve the reliability of the results?

A Use boiled ATP to prove the action was not due to enzyme function.

B Repeat the experiment several times.

C Use another strand with water as a control.

D Use a sucrose solution instead of a glucose solution.

27. Which of the following features of a pesticide would make it most suitable for use on crops?

	Effect on pest	*Length of action*	*Persistence in soil*	*Effect on host plant*
A	specific	short	remains a long time	some damage
B	non-specific	long	remains a very short time	harmless
C	specific	short	remains a very short time	harmless
D	non-specific	short	remains a very long time	little damage

28. The following factors may lead to desertification.

1. The expanding human population putting pressure on land for food production
2. Top soils dry up and are quickly blown away by wind
3. Sand starts to invade marginal land from desert areas nearby
4. Forests are cleared to generate supplies of fuel and materials for building

The correct order for these is

A 1, 2, 3, 4

B 2, 4, 3, 1

C 1, 4, 2, 3

D 3, 4, 2, 1

29. Serious epidemics of potentially fatal diseases seldom occur. Which of the following reasons has **not** contributed to this?

A Vaccination programmes

B Improved water supplies

C Availability of organised assistance

D Lower standards of living

30. Which of the following greenhouse gases has the most damaging effect on the atmosphere?

A Nitrous oxide

B Carbon dioxide

C Methane

D Fluorocarbons (CFCs)

DO NOT WRITE IN THIS MARGIN

SECTION B

All questions in this section should be attempted.

MARKS

1. The diagram below shows some of the organelles found in a human cell.

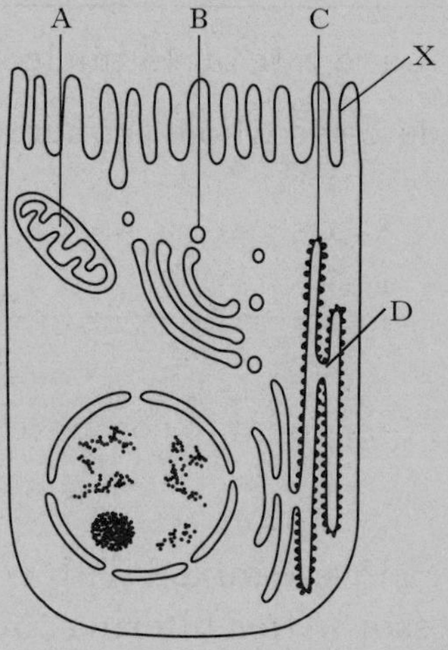

(*a*) Complete the table below by inserting the correct letter, name and function. **3**

Letter	*Name*	*Function*
		provides ATP
	secretory vesicle	
D		protein synthesis

(*b*) (i) Indicate on the diagram, by means of a line labelled P, the position of a nuclear pore. **1**

(ii) Give one function of nuclear pores. ______________________

____ **1**

(*c*) What is the significance of the highly folded membrane at X?

____ **1**

2. (*a*) A sequence of bases on part of an mRNA molecule reads as follows:

AUAAUACUUCAAGAGCUUGAGGAGGAGCUU

There are 4 different amino acids in the protein coded for by this section of mRNA: isoleucine (Ile), leucine (Leu), glutamic acid (Glu) and glutamine (Gln). Only one glutamine is present.

Complete the following diagram to show the amino acid sequence using the abbreviations given. **2**

Ile				Glu					

(*b*) Give the tRNA anticodons for the following sequence of amino acids.

Amino acids	Isoleucine	Glutamic acid	Leucine
tRNA			

1

DO NOT WRITE IN THIS MARGIN

2. (continued)

MARKS

(*c*) Give **two** ways in which mRNA is different from DNA.

1 ____

2 ____ 1

(*d*) This cell can translate mRNA at a rate of 45 nucleotides per second.

How long will it take to translate the whole sequence of RNA shown?

Space for calculation

____________________ seconds 1

3. A student designed the following experiment to compare the activity of catalase in different plant materials.

Equal masses of each plant material were mixed with equal volumes of water and then blended in a food processor. After filtering the extracts, the student took 2 cm^3 of each extract and added this to 5 cm^3 of hydrogen peroxide. The volume of oxygen given off within a set time was measured and converted into a "relative activity" value. The higher the relative activity value, the more oxygen was released. This was repeated once more and the results are shown below as the "relative activity" for each plant material.

Plant source	*Relative activity*		
	1	*2*	*Average*
Potato	1·0	0·8	
Leek	3·5	3·9	
Parsnip	6·6	6·8	
Radish	0·5	0·2	

(*a*) Complete the table by calculating the average activity for these plants. 1

(*b*) Draw a **bar chart** to show the **average** activity for each plant source. 2

DO NOT WRITE IN THIS MARGIN

MARKS

3. (continued)

(*c*) (i) How could the reliability of this experiment be improved?

____

____ **1**

(ii) State **one** variable which would need to be controlled to improve the validity of any conclusions.

____ **1**

(iii) Suggest a suitable control for this experiment.

____ **1**

4. In humans, the ability to taste the chemical phenylthiocarbamide (PTC) is controlled by a gene. Tasters have at least one dominant allele while non-tasters are homozygous recessive.

The diagram below shows the inheritance of this trait in a family.

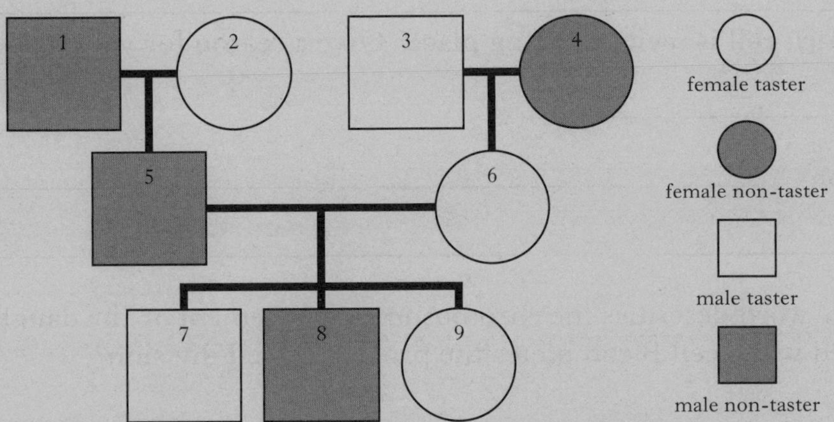

(*a*) (i) Using the symbols T to represent the allele for tasting and t to represent the allele for non-tasting, state the genotypes of individuals 1 and 6

1 ____________________ 6 ____________________ **1**

(ii) How many people, shown on the diagram, are homozygous recessive?

____________________ **1**

(iii) Which individual genotype cannot be known for certain?

____

Explain your answer. ______________________________

____ **2**

____

(*b*) Explain the term **polygenic inheritance**.

____

____ **1**

DO NOT WRITE IN THIS MARGIN

MARKS

5. The diagrams below show two human cells in which division of the nucleus is taking place.

For simplicity, only four chromosomes are shown.

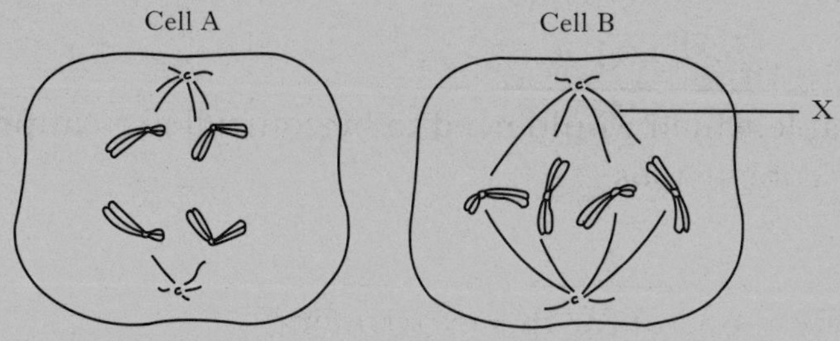

(*a*) (i) How many chromatids are present in cell A? ______________ **1**

(ii) What is structure X called? Give a function for this structure in cell B.

X ______________

Function ______________

______________ **2**

(iii) In which cell is meiosis taking place? Give a reason for your answer.

Cell ______________

Reason ______________

______________ **2**

(*b*) What single word describes the chromosome complement of the daughter cells formed when cell B completes the process of cell division?

______________ **1**

(*c*) Where in the body does meiosis occur? ______________ **1**

6. The diagram below shows some of the events associated with ovulation in humans.

Approximately halfway through the cycle, event A takes place.

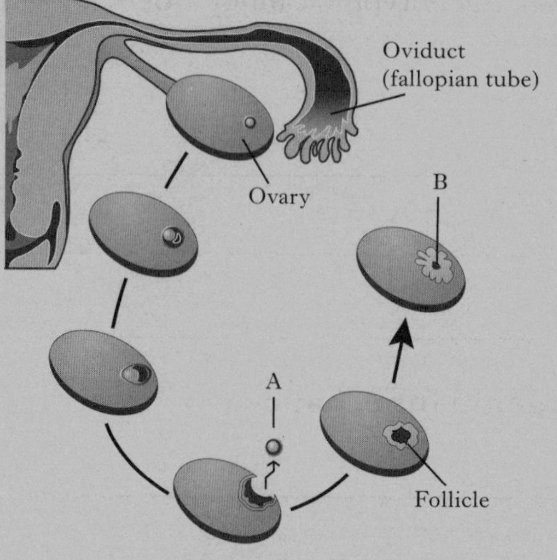

DO NOT WRITE IN THIS MARGIN

6. (continued)

MARKS

(*a*) (i) What term describes event A? ______________________ 1

(ii) A sudden rise in which hormone causes event A to take place?

______________________ 1

(iii) Which gland secretes this hormone? ______________________ 1

(iv) Name structure B. Name two hormones secreted by this structure.

Structure B ______________________

1 ______________________ 2 ______________________ 2

(v) Indicate on the diagram, by means of the letter X, the normal site for implantation of a fertilised egg. 1

(*b*) Explain what is meant by *in vitro* fertilisation.

____

____ 2

7. The diagram below shows the human heart and part of its conducting system.

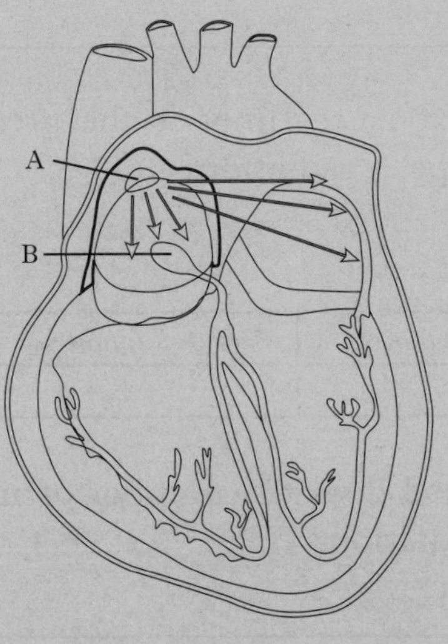

(*a*) (i) Indicate on the diagram, by using the letter P, the chamber within which the pressure of the blood reaches its highest level. 1

(ii) Name the parts labelled A and B.

A ______________________ B ______________________ 2

(iii) Explain the function of part A in the cardiac cycle.

____

____

____ 1

(*b*) What term is used to describe the heart when it is in a resting state?

______________________ 1

DO NOT WRITE IN THIS MARGIN

MARKS

8. During a nuclear power plant accident, some humans were exposed to two different types of radiation, type A and type B. The graphs below show the effects of the length of exposure on the number of mutations per person.

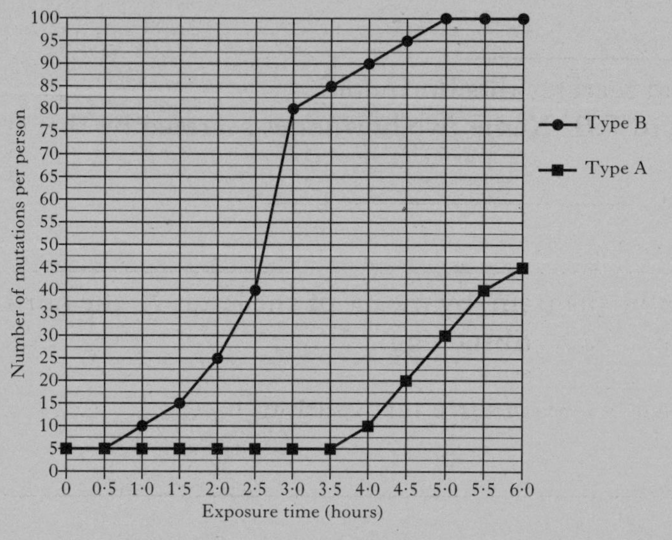

(*a*) Why is the number of mutations per person not zero, even when there is no exposure?

____

____ **1**

(*b*) Between which range of exposure times is the greatest increase in the number of mutations for type A radiation?

Tick the box.

2·0–3·0 hours	*3·0–4·0 hours*	*4·0–5·0 hours*	*5·0–6·0 hours*

1

(*c*) Over which 30-minute period does the number of mutations per person increase by 40 for type B radiation?

____ **1**

(*d*) (i) Which radiation is most dangerous?

Type ____________________________________ **1**

(ii) Give **two** reasons for your answer

Reason 1 __________________________________

____

Reason 2 __________________________________

____ **2**

DO NOT WRITE IN THIS MARGIN

MARKS

8. (continued)

(*e*) (i) State the types of gene mutation shown in the following two examples.

DNA	*Nucleotide sequence*	*Type of mutation*
NORMAL	ACG CCA CTC	
ALTERED	AAC GCC ACT C	
NORMAL	ACG CCA CTC	
ALTERED	ACG GCA CTC	

2

(ii) Which **one** of these two types of mutation would have the greatest effect on the structure of the protein which is made? Explain your answer.

Type of mutation ____________________

Explanation ____________________

____

____________________ 2

9. The following diagram shows part of a capillary bed.

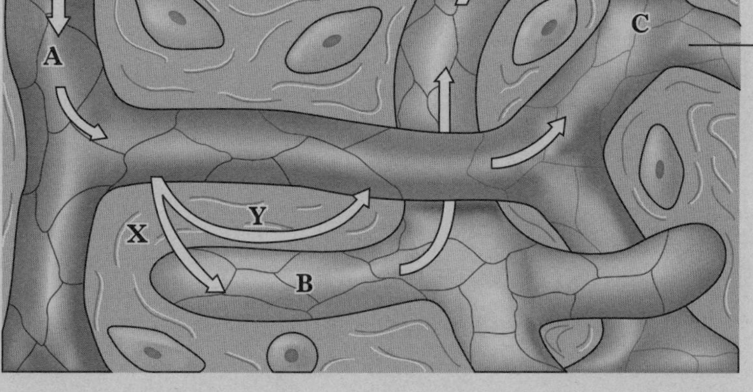

(*a*) Match the names of the structures with the letters shown.

Structure	*Letter*
Arteriole	
Venule	
Lymph vessel	

1

(*b*) Describe what is happening at each of the points labelled X and Y.

X ____________________

____

Y ____________________

____________________ 2

(*c*) Why does the pressure of blood fall as it moves from A to C?

____

____________________ 1

9. (continued)

MARKS

(*d*) Name the process allows oxygen to move out of structure A into the surrounding tissue cells.

_______________ 1

(*e*) What is the function of valves in lymph vessels?

_______________ 1

10. The following question relates to patterns of smoking in a part of England. Data collected in 2000 were compared with data from an equal-size sample from 1990. In 2008, the socio-economic groups (A, B and C) of 1000 smokers were recorded.

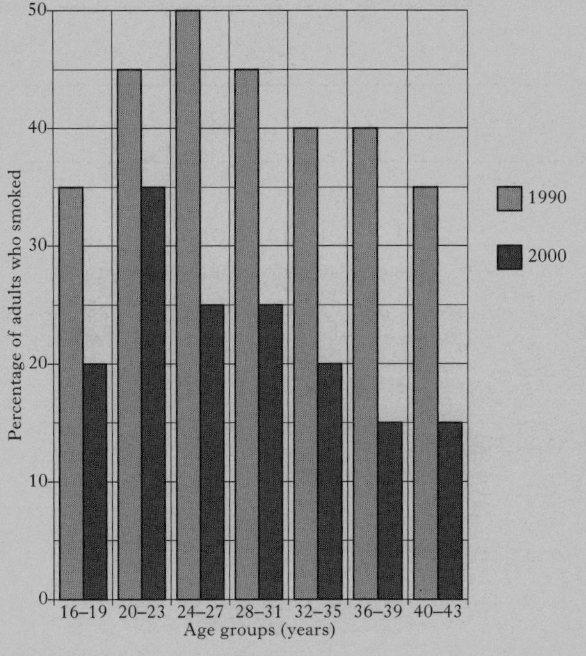

Figure 1 Percentage of adults in different age groups who smoked

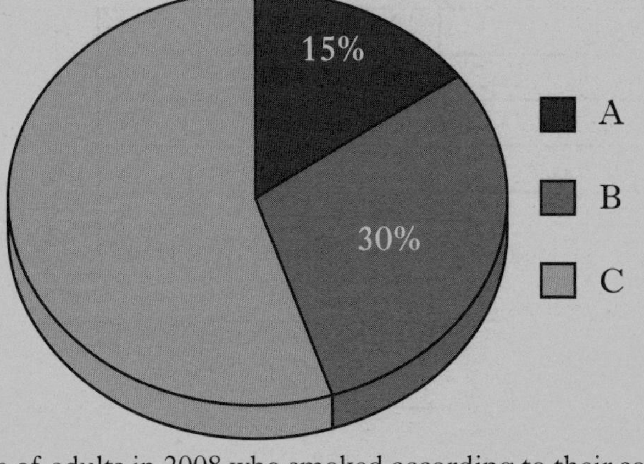

Figure 2 Percentage of adults in 2008 who smoked according to their socio-economic groups

(*a*) From **Figure 1**, compare the pattern of smoking in adults between the ages of 16 and 27 for the two different years sampled.

____

____

_______________ 2

DO NOT WRITE IN THIS MARGIN

10. (continued)

MARKS

(*b*) From **Figure 1**, express the percentage of adults aged 36–39 who smoked in the two different years sampled as a **simple, whole number** ratio.

__________ : __________ 1

(*c*) From **Figure 2**, suggest **one** reason why, in the sample taken for 2008, the smallest percentage of smokers came from socio-economic group A.

____

____

______________________________ 1

(*d*) Approximately 20% of group C in the 2008 sample were women. From **Figure 2**, calculate the number of men in the manual group who smoked.

Space for calculation

__________ 1

(*e*) Suggest **two** ways in which the data shown here do not allow valid conclusions to be drawn.

1 ______________________________

____

2 ______________________________

______________________________ 2

(*f*) Data such as is shown here can be useful to health agencies. Give **one** way in which these agencies might benefit from such results.

____

______________________________ 1

DO NOT WRITE IN THIS MARGIN

MARKS

11. The diagram below shows part of the human nervous system.

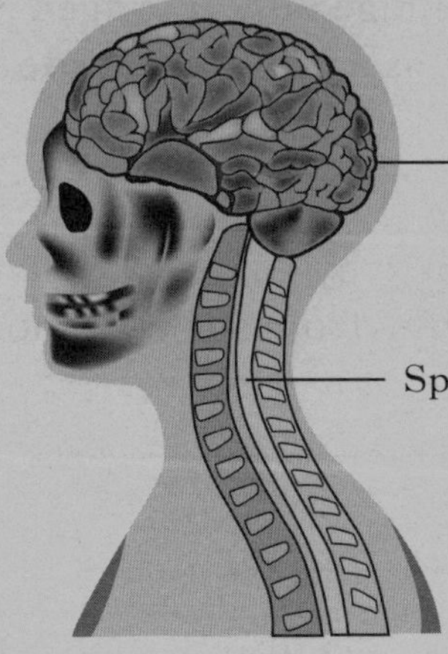

(*a*) What is the name give to this branch of the human nervous system?

____ **1**

(*b*) Which part of the human nervous system controls heart rate?

____ **1**

(*c*) What type of cell, found in the spinal cord, carries impulses towards muscles?

____ **1**

(*d*) Insert the terms in the list below into the correct boxes to show the direction of flow of a nerve impulse.

cell body – effector - axon - dendrites - receptor

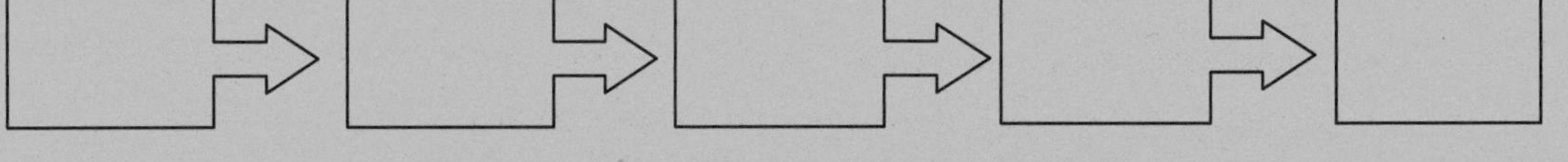

2

(*e*) Some nerves can carry impulses at a rate of 120 m/second. A person is 2·8 m tall. Assuming this rate of transmission, how long would it take for an impulse to travel the length of the body?

____________________ seconds **1**

DO NOT WRITE IN THIS MARGIN

MARKS

12. The man shown in the diagram below is a "split-brain" person whose *corpus callosum* has been surgically cut, separating his left and right cerebral hemispheres. He was asked to focus on a white spot in the middle of a screen then quickly shown the two images at the same time so that each image goes to the opposite hemisphere.

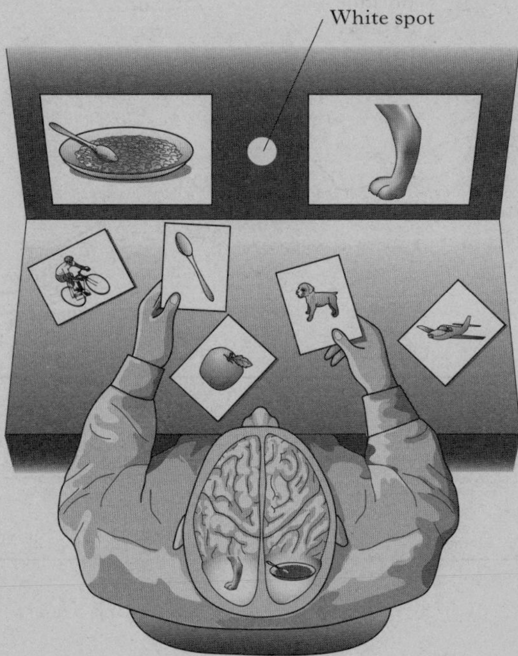

(*a*) What is the function of the *corpus callosum*?

____

____ **1**

(*b*) (i) The man was asked to say what he saw. What would he answer?

____ **1**

(ii) Now he was asked to lift up a card which corresponded to what he saw. Which card would he pick up?

____ **1**

DO NOT WRITE IN THIS MARGIN

MARKS

13. The diagram below shows a small reservoir in which the fish stock is declining, and some surrounding land.

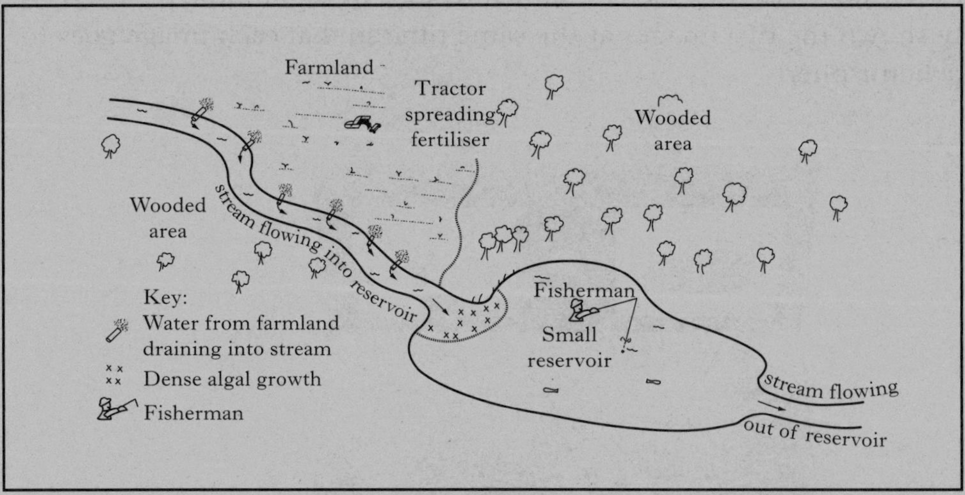

(*a*) What pollutant is likely to be added to the stream through the draining from the farmland?

____ **1**

(*b*) What event could take place which would increase the rate of drainage of the pollutant into the stream?

____ **1**

(*c*) What term is used to describe the dense algal growth?

____ **1**

(*d*) Explain why there would be a decline in the fish population in the reservoir.

____

____

____ **2**

DO NOT WRITE IN THIS MARGIN

SECTION C

MARKS

Both questions in this section should be attempted.

Note that each question contains a choice.

Labelled diagrams may be used where appropriate.

1. Answer **either** A **or** B.

A. The body uses a variety of compounds other than glucose as sources of energy in some circumstances. Discuss this statement under the following headings:

(i) marathon running; **5**

(ii) starvation. **5**

OR **(10)**

B. Discuss immunity under the following headings:

(i) allergy; **6**

(ii) autoimmunity. **4**

(10)

In question 2, ONE mark is available for coherence and ONE mark is available for relevance.

2. Answer **either** A **or** B.

A. The temperature of the body is regulated despite changes in the environment. Discuss how this regulation is achieved and what results from loss of this stability. **(10)**

OR

B. Discuss some of the possible harmful effects on the environment of increasing the levels of atmospheric carbon dioxide. **(10)**

[End of question paper]

Exam 2

Leckie × Leckie
Scotland's leading educational publishers

Answer sheet for Section A:

Higher Human Biology
Practice Papers for SQA Exams

Please select your answer using a single mark e.g. A ☐ B ■ C ☐ D ☐

	A	B	C	D
1.	☐	☐	☐	☐
2.	☐	☐	☐	☐
3.	☐	☐	☐	☐
4.	☐	☐	☐	☐
5.	☐	☐	☐	☐
6.	☐	☐	☐	☐
7.	☐	☐	☐	☐
8.	☐	☐	☐	☐
9.	☐	☐	☐	☐
10.	☐	☐	☐	☐
11.	☐	☐	☐	☐
12.	☐	☐	☐	☐
13.	☐	☐	☐	☐
14.	☐	☐	☐	☐
15.	☐	☐	☐	☐
16.	☐	☐	☐	☐
17.	☐	☐	☐	☐
18.	☐	☐	☐	☐
19.	☐	☐	☐	☐
20.	☐	☐	☐	☐
21.	☐	☐	☐	☐
22.	☐	☐	☐	☐
23.	☐	☐	☐	☐
24.	☐	☐	☐	☐
25.	☐	☐	☐	☐
26.	☐	☐	☐	☐
27.	☐	☐	☐	☐
28.	☐	☐	☐	☐
29.	☐	☐	☐	☐
30.	☐	☐	☐	☐

Higher Human Biology

Practice Papers
for SQA Exams

Time allowed:
1 hour 45 minutes

Exam 2

Fill in these boxes and read what is printed below.

Full name of school	Town

Forename(s)	Surname

Read each question carefully.

Attempt **all** questions.

Write your answers on the blank paper provided.

Write as neatly as possible.

Answer in sentences wherever possible.

Leckie × Leckie
Scotland's leading educational publishers

Read closely

1. For Section A, you should use an HB pencil and, where neccesary, a rubber.
2. Each Answer is **either** A, B, C or D. When you have decided your answer, use your pencil to put a line in the appropriate space on the answer sheet. (See the example below.)
3. Each question has **only one correct** answer.
4. Do not do any rough working on the answer sheet: use a separate sheet of paper.

Sample question

The surface area:volume ratio of a cube with edges 1 cm is

A 1:1

B 3:1

C 6:1

D 12:1

The correct answer is **C** – 6:1. This answer has been clearly marked in **pencil** below.

Changing an answer

If you need to change an answer, carefully rub out your original, then use your pencil to fill in the answer you now want. Below, the answer has been changed to **D**.

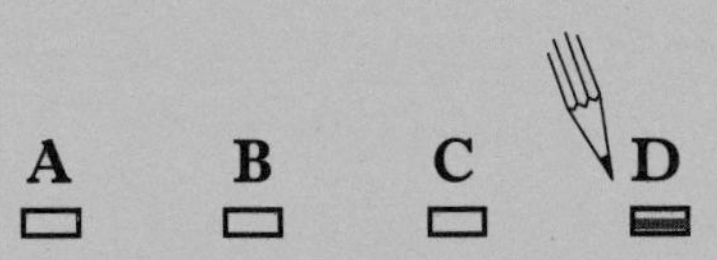

SECTION A

All questions in this section should be attempted.
Answers should be given on the separate answer sheet provided.

1. Which cell structure is shown in the diagram below?

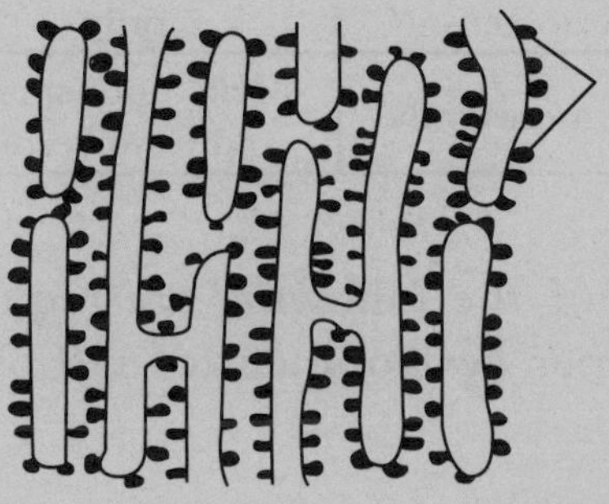

A Smooth endoplasmic reticulum

B Rough endoplasmic reticulum

C Golgi apparatus

D Cristae of mitochondria

2. Which of the following will contain a great deal of the proteins actin and myosin?

A Brain

B Biceps muscle

C Humerus

D Retina

3. An example of phagocytosis is

A diffusion of oxygen into the lungs

B passing of an enzyme out through a cell membrane

C taking in minute quantities of liquids across a cell membrane

D a white blood cell surrounding a bacterium.

4. Which of the following does **not** contain the element nitrogen?

A Starch

B Lipase

C Ammonia

D Glucagon

5. The following table shows the percentage of men and women in a part of Britain who survived two different types of cancer for at least one year after diagnosis.

Type of cancer	*Sex*	*1971–1975*	*1976–1980*	*1981–1985*	*1986–1990*
oesophagus	*males*	12	13	17	22
	females	16	17	23	26
stomach	*males*	13	14	20	25
	females	15	16	22	27

Which of the following statements is **false**? Over the period of the study

A survival rates for men with stomach cancer have increased more than those for men with cancer of the oesophagus

B women have less chance of surviving stomach cancer compared to men

C fewer people survived cancer of the oesophagus than stomach cancer in the period 1986–1990

D in men, the greatest increase in survival was for stomach cancer between the periods 1976–1980 and 1981–1985.

6. The diagram below shows an experiment which was set up and left for 3 hours.

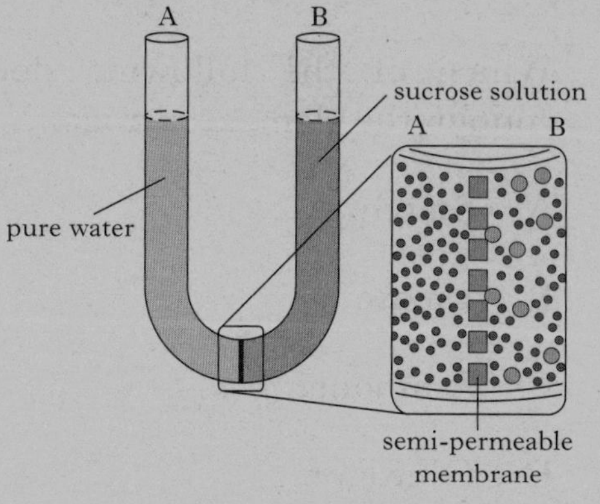

After 3 hours, which of the following results is **true**?

A The levels in both A and B would remain the same.

B The level in A would be higher than in B.

C Sucrose molecules would be found in tubes A and B.

D Sucrose molecules would be found only in tube B.

7. The diagram below shows how a gene for a human disease is passed on in a family.

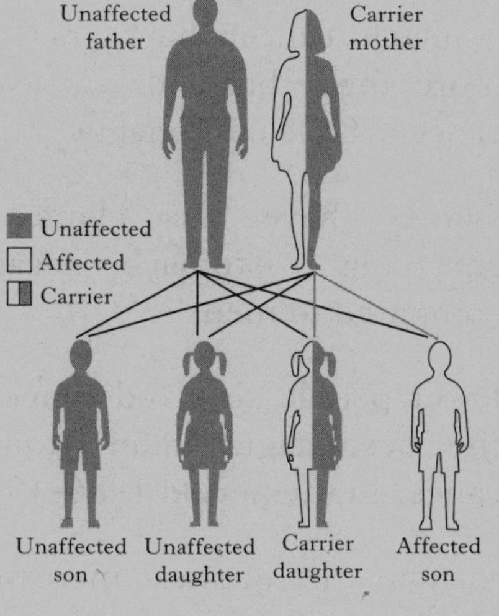

The allele for this disease is

A dominant and not sex-linked

B dominant and sex-linked

C recessive and not sex-linked

D recessive and sex-linked.

8. Which of the following is **correct**?

	Seminiferous tubules	*Interstitial cells*
A	Make sperm	Make testosterone
B	Make testosterone	Make sperm
C	Make both sperm and testosterone	Make testosterone only
D	Make sperm only	Make both sperm and testosterone

9. Which of the following are required for proper development of red blood cells?

A Vitamin B_{12} and iron

B Vitamin B_{12} and vitamin C

C Vitamin C and iron

D Iron and magnesium

10. The diagram below shows part of the human circulatory system.

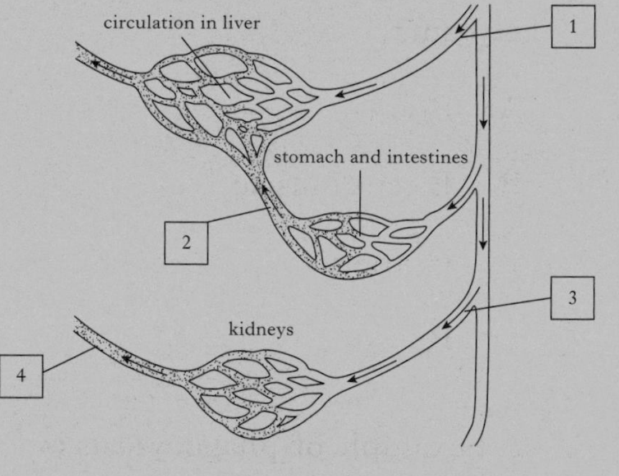

Which of the following is **correct**?

	Hepatic artery	*Hepatic portal vein*	*Renal artery*	*Renal vein*
A	1	2	3	4
B	2	3	4	1
C	3	2	1	4
D	1	3	4	2

11. Which of the following hormones is produced by the pituitary gland?

A Glucagon

B Insulin

C Antidiuretic hormone

D Adrenaline

12. A baby may receive antibodies in its mother's milk during the early stages of breast-feeding.

This is an example of

A naturally acquired active immunity

B naturally acquired passive immunity

C artificially acquired active immunity

D artificially acquired passive immunity.

13. A person's systole lasts 0·2 seconds and diastole 0·4 seconds.

What is the heart rate of this person in beats per minute?

A 75

B 100

C 125

D 150

14. Which of the following blood groups can receive blood from a person whose group is AB?

A O and B

B A and B

C O and A

D AB only

15. Very young babies are more liable to feel the effects of the cold than older children.

The reason for this is young babies have a

A high rate of metabolism

B low rate of metabolism

C high surface area to volume ratio

D low surface area to volume ratio.

Questions 16 and 17 refer to the following graph.

Some years ago a study was conducted into a hospital which admitted very sick babies. The hospital was located in a developing country. The percentage mortality was plotted against age groups.

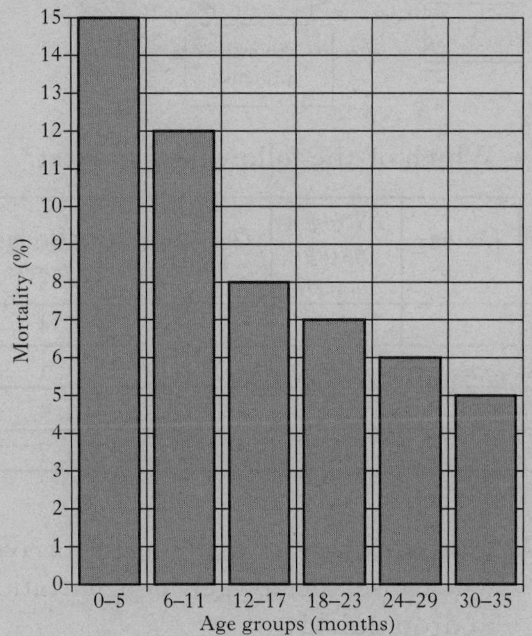

16. In the 6–11 month age group, the sample size was 1300. How many of these children survived?

A 143

B 286

C 572

D 1144

17. 500 babies aged 0–5 months were admitted. How many of these babies did not survive?

A 5

B 20

C 50

D 75

18. The following diagram shows the nitrogen cycle.

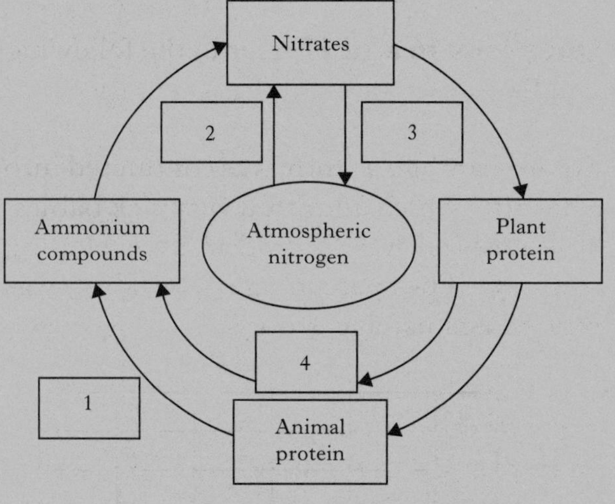

Which of the following is correct?

	Decom-posers	*Nitrogen fixing bacteria*	*Denitrifying bacteria*	*Decom-posers*
A	1	2	3	4
B	2	3	4	1
C	3	2	1	4
D	1	3	4	2

19. Untreated sewage escaping into a river will cause the oxygen concentration to drop quickly.

The reason for this is that

A algae increase to form blooms which use up oxygen

B bacteria multiply rapidly and use up the oxygen as they respire

C levels of nutrients in the water fall

D fish multiply and use up the oxygen.

Questions 20 and 21 refer to the following graph.

The graph shows the change in body temperature of two people, one aged 18 years and one aged 85 years, during exposure to an environmental air temperature of 15 °C. No form of insulating clothing was worn during this experiment.

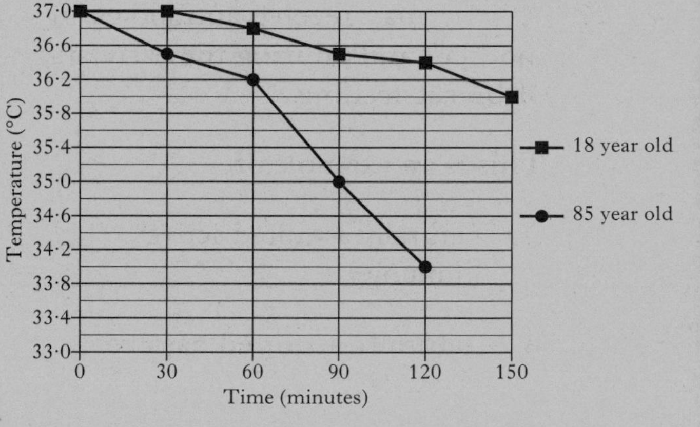

20. When the body temperature drops below 35 °C, hypothermia sets in.

How long would it take the 85 year old to develop hypothermia?

A 30 minutes

B 60 minutes

C 90 minutes

D 120 minutes

21. If the drop in temperature of the 18 year old continued at the rate it did from 120 to 150 minutes, what do you predict would be his temperature after 180 minutes?

A 34·0 °C

B 34·6 °C

C 35·0 °C

D 35·6 °C

22. The diagram below shows a part of the human excretory system highly magnified.

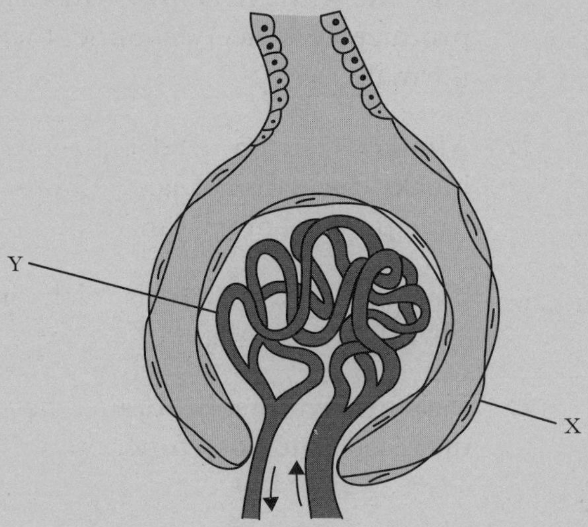

The structures indicated by the letters X and Y are

	X	*Y*
A	glomerulus	nephron
B	nephron	Bowman's capsule
C	Bowman's capsule	glomerulus
D	capillaries	nephron

23. A child dressing up in an adult's clothing is called

A imitation

B generalisation

C motivation

D discrimination.

24. A girl is very relaxed with a friend's dog which she knows well. However, when presented with a stranger's pet Alsatian, she is afraid.

This is an example of

A generalisation

B shaping

C imitation

D discrimination.

Questions 25 and 26 refer to the graph below.

The graph shows the recommended daily calorie intake for males of different ages.

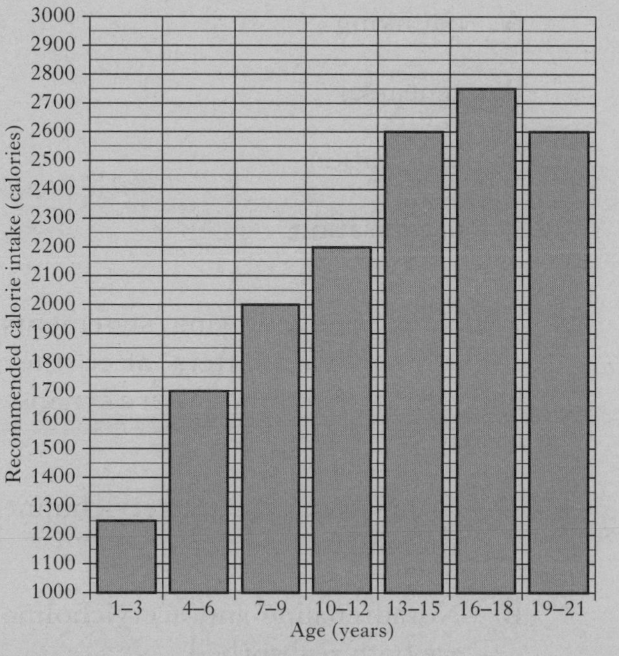

25. What is the percentage increase in recommended calorie intake from age 10–12 to 13–15 years?

A 9

B 10

C 12

D 18

26. What are the recommended calorie intakes for ages 1–3, 4–6 and 7–9 expressed as a **simple whole number ratio**?

A 1250:1700:2000

B 125:170:200

C 25:34:40

D 12:17:20

27. A student improved his ability to remember an important telephone number by going over it several times in his head.

This process is called

A chunking

B rehearsal

C elaboration

D organisation.

28. Which of the following statements about neurotransmitters after they have served their function at a synapse is **true**?

A Noradrenaline and acetylcholine are both broken down.

B Noradrenaline and acetylcholine are both reabsorbed.

C Noradrenaline is broken down enzymatically, acetylcholine is reabsorbed.

D Noradrenaline is reabsorbed, acetylcholine is broken down enzymatically.

29. Which of the following is **not** evidence of a molecular basis for memory?

A Patients with Alzheimer's disease produce less acetylcholine than normal.

B Monkeys given a drug which blocks the action of acetylcholine have poor memory function.

C The limbic system is rich in NMDA receptors.

D Patients with split brains have decreased memory function.

30. An RNA nucleotide could be formed from phosphate with

A ribose and uracil

B ribose and thymine

C deoxyribose and uracil

D deoxyribose and thymine.

DO NOT WRITE IN THIS MARGIN

SECTION B

All questions in this section should be attempted.

MARKS

1. The diagram below shows part of an enzyme-catalysed pathway in humans. A is the normal pathway while pathway B causes an accumulation of substance X which in turn affects the proper brain development of a baby soon after it is born.

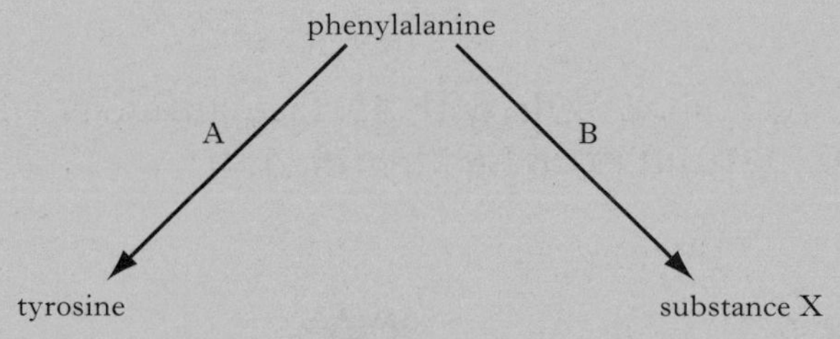

(*a*) Why does substance X build up in the blood of babies if pathway A is not working?

______________________________________ **1**

(*b*) Substance X, if allowed to accumulate, can cause phenylketonuria.

Why does substance X not build up in the blood of the baby before it is born?

____

______________________________________ **1**

(*c*) How can phenylketonuria be treated?

____

______________________________________ **1**

(*d*) (i) This condition, in which an enzyme is missing or not working properly, is present at birth

What is the general name for conditions such as this?

______________________________________ **1**

(ii) Give another example of such a condition.

______________________________________ **1**

(*e*) In the UK, babies have their blood tested almost immediately after they are born to check the levels of phenylalanine in their blood.

What term is used to describe the testing of babies very soon after they are born?

______________________________________ **1**

DO NOT WRITE IN THIS MARGIN

MARKS

1. (continued)

(*f*) (i) Where will excess amino acids, such as tyrosine, normally be broken down in the body?

____ **1**

(ii) What is this process called?

____ **1**

2. The diagram below shows red blood cells with surface antigens which allow the four blood groups, A, B, AB and O, to be identified.

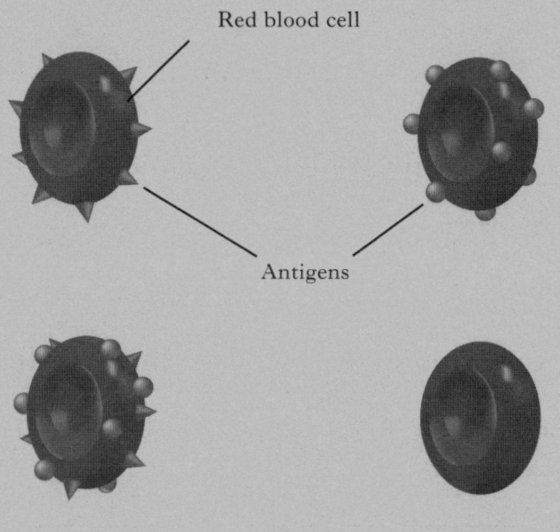

(*a*) Complete the table below to show the antigens present on the red blood cells and the antibodies present in the plasma of the four blood groups.

Blood group	*Antigens present on surface of red blood cells*	*Antibodies present in the plasma*
A		antibody-B
B		
AB		
O	Neither antigen	

2

(*b*) Which blood group(s) could be transfused into a person whose blood group is AB?

____ **1**

(*c*) Blood group O is sometimes referred to as the universal donor.

Explain the meaning of this term.

____ **1**

DO NOT WRITE IN THIS MARGIN

2. (continued)

MARKS

(*d*) (i) The concentration of the various dissolved substances in plasma is kept within very narrow limits.

Explain how this helps to keep the shape of the red blood cells. **1**

(ii) Explain the importance of the shape of red blood cells. **1**

3. A number of sweet molecules have been made artificially and are permitted for use in human consumption. They are referred to by their E-numbers.

Table 1 shows some of these sweet molecules along with their potencies, which is a measure of how sweet the additive is compared to ordinary table sugar, sucrose. Sucrose has a potency of 1.

Table 1

Sweet molecule (E-number)	*Potency (sucrose = 1)*
950	200
951	200
952	30
954	300

(*a*) Draw a **bar chart** to show these data. **2**

DO NOT WRITE IN THIS MARGIN

MARKS

3. (continued)

(*b*) A recent safety evaluation recommended that E952 in food should not exceed 7 mg per kg of body weight.

What would be the maximum intake for a man who weighs 65 kg?

Space for calculation

____________________ mg **1**

(*c*) The Food Standards Agency recommends that parents of very young children who drink diluting drinks which contain E952 should … dilute them more than they would for an adult.

Give **one** possible reason for this advice.

____

____

____ **1**

4. The diagram below shows stages in aerobic respiration.

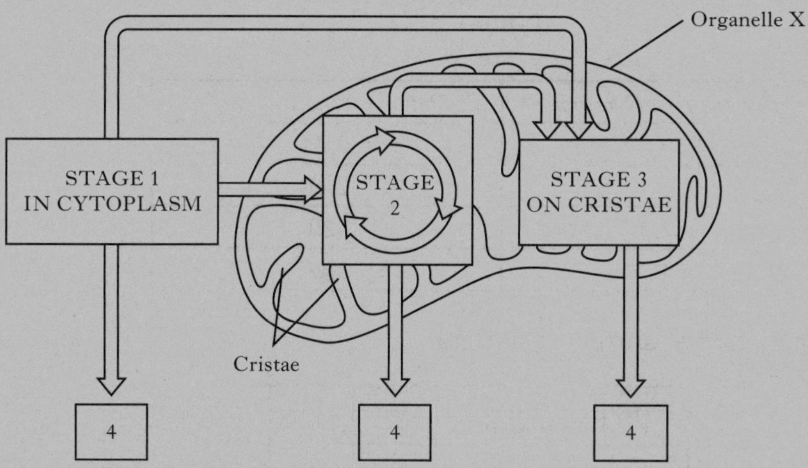

(*a*) Name each stage.

Stage 1 ______________________________

Stage 2 ______________________________

Stage 3 ______________________________ **2**

(*b*) Name organelle X where stages 2 and 3 take place.

____ **1**

DO NOT WRITE IN THIS MARGIN

4. (continued)

MARKS

(*c*) What is transferred between

Stage 1 and stage 2? ______________________

Stage 2 and stage 3? ______________________ **2**

(*d*) What chemical, represented by the boxes numbered 4, is formed?

______________________ **1**

(*e*) What is the main respiratory substrate used in human cells?

______________________ **1**

5. The following information refers to genetic diseases in humans.

Duchenne muscular dystrophy is sex-linked.

Huntington's disease is caused by an autosomal dominant allele.

Cystic fibrosis is an autosomal recessive disease.

The family tree below shows an inheritance pattern of one of these conditions.

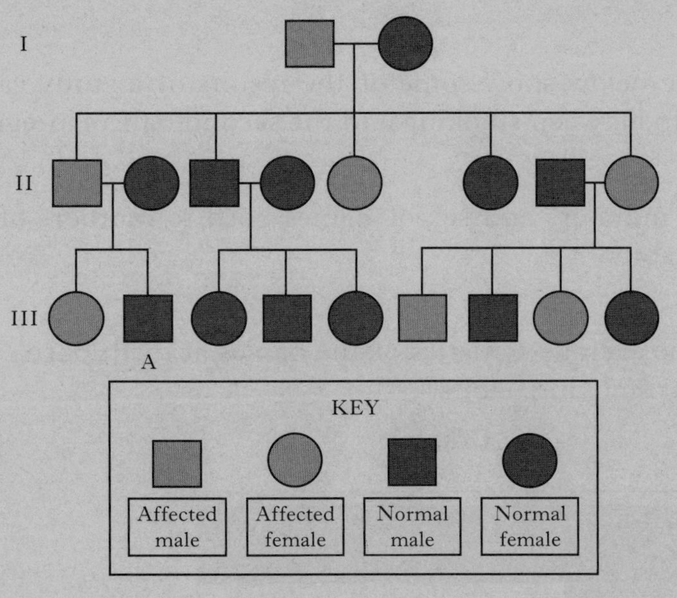

(*a*) Which of the three conditions are most likely to be shown by this diagram? Give **two** reasons for your answer.

Condition ______________________ **1**

Reason 1 ______________________

____

Reason 2 ______________________

______________________ **2**

5. (continued)

MARKS

(*b*) What is the probability that individual A is heterozygous?

Space for calculation

______________% **1**

(*c*) The frequency of this disease is approximately 1 in 10,000. In a population of 5,000,000, approximately half are males and half are females. How many females are likely to have this disease?

Space for calculation

______________ **1**

(*d*) Amniocentesis allows material from the developing fetus to be examined for abnormalities in the chromosomes.

State **one** other procedure which can be used for this type of pre-natal testing.

____ **1**

6. The graph and table below show some of the results of a study carried into the relationship between smoking and the second half of pregnancy.

Graph 1 shows the numbers and sex of babies born to mothers of different smoking habits.

Table 1 shows some average statistics of the babies at birth born to mothers of different smoking habits.

Graph 1

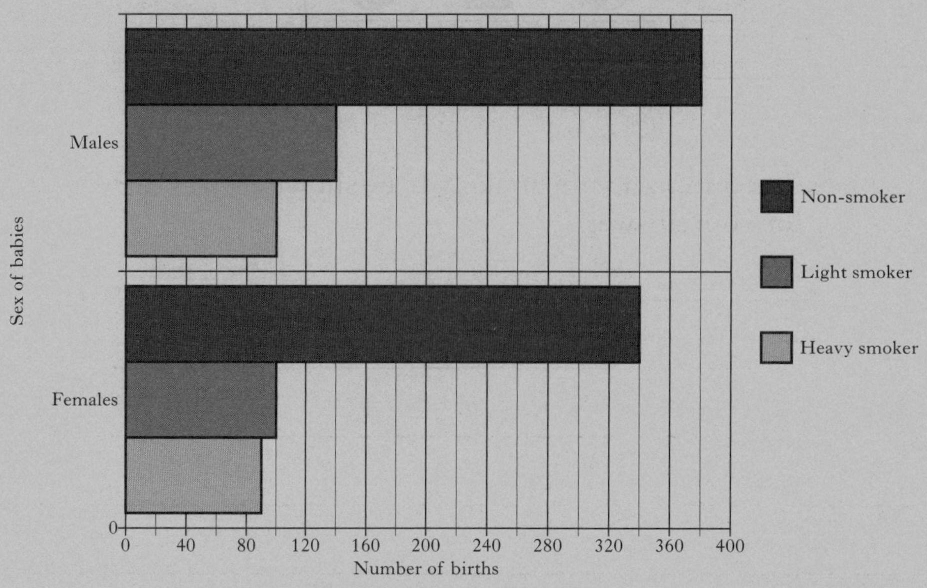

DO NOT WRITE IN THIS MARGIN

6. (continued)

MARKS

Table 1

Statistic	*Non-smoker*	*Light smoker*	*Heavy smoker*
Birth mass (kg)	3·45	3·25	3·16
Circumference of head (cms)	36·00	35·80	35·60
Length (cms)	52·00	51·40	51·40

(*a*) Assuming all the pregnancies started at the same time, how long did the study last?

____________________________________ 1

(*b*) How many babies in total were examined?

Space for calculation

__________ 1

(*c*) What was the percentage of mothers who were light smokers?

Space for calculation

__________% 1

(*d*) Which of the statistics measured is affected most when the mothers smoke heavily?

____________________________________ 1

(*e*) State **two** trends shown by the babies of mothers who do not smoke.

1 ____________________________________

____

2 ____________________________________

____________________________________ 2

(*f*) How could the reliability of the results have been improved?

____

____________________________________ 1

(*g*) Suggest **one** use which might be made of results from studies such as this.

____

____

____________________________________ 1

DO NOT WRITE IN THIS MARGIN

MARKS

7. The diagram below shows a stage in the development of a human fetus.

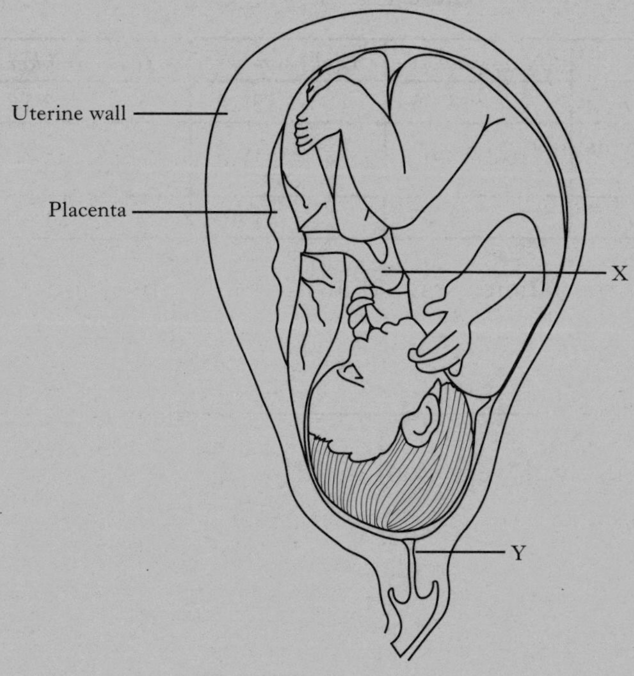

(*a*) Identify structures X and Y.

X ______________________ Y ______________________ 1

(*b*) State **two** beneficial functions of the placenta.

1 ______________________

____

2 ______________________

______________________ 2

(*c*) Give **one** example of a harmful substance which could travel from a mother to her developing fetus along the umbilical cord.

______________________ 1

(*d*) Which hormone stimulates the cells lining structure Y to produce watery mucus to allow sperm to penetrate more easily?

______________________ 1

DO NOT WRITE IN THIS MARGIN

MARKS

8. An experiment was carried out in the late 1970s to study how learning a language could be improved. Groups of English speakers were presented with a series of words in another language, their meanings in English and images of objects whose names sounded like the foreign words.

Here is an example of the technique.

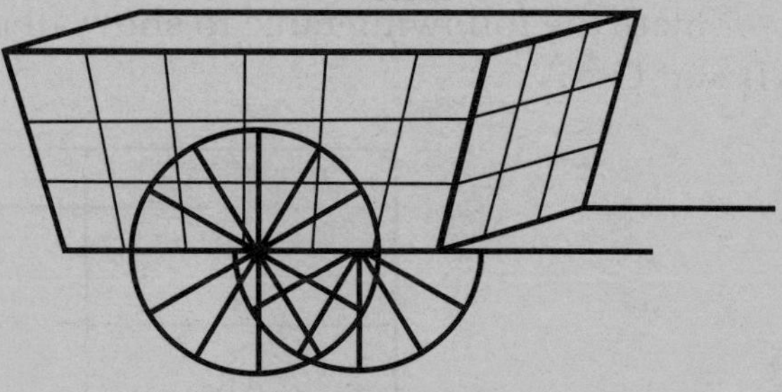

carta	***letter***	
Spanish word	Meaning in English	Image

One test group was given 120 Russian words to learn in this way while a second test group, a control, was given the same list but with no named images. The experimental group did 50% better when asked to recall the meanings immediately after the test compared with the control group.

(*a*) What does this experiment suggest about how we can improve our memory of foreign words and their meanings?

____

______________________________ **1**

(*b*) How could these results be made more reliable?

______________________________ **1**

(*c*) Describe **one** other way control group that could be set up.

____

______________________________ **1**

(*d*) Suggest one limitation of learning a list of foreign words in this way.

____

______________________________ **1**

DO NOT WRITE IN THIS MARGIN

MARKS

9. Blood groups in humans are controlled by three alleles, A, B and O. A and B are equally dominant and both are dominant over O.

(*a*) What term is used to describe the situation in which a gene has two or more alleles?

______________________________ **1**

(*b*) Complete the following table to show all the genotypes of blood groups A, AB and O.

Blood group	*Genotype(s)*
A	
AB	
O	

2

(*c*) If a group **AB** man marries a group **O** woman, what are the possible blood groups for their children?

Space for calculation

______________________________ **1**

(*d*) What is meant by **agglutination** of red blood cells?

______________________________ **1**

(*e*) **Immunosuppressor drugs** are often given to patients who have had a transplant.

Give **one** advantage and **one** disadvantage of such drugs.

Advantage ______________________________

____

Disadvantage ______________________________

______________________________ **2**

DO NOT WRITE IN THIS MARGIN

MARKS

10. The diagram below shows part of the system by which glucose is regulated in the body.

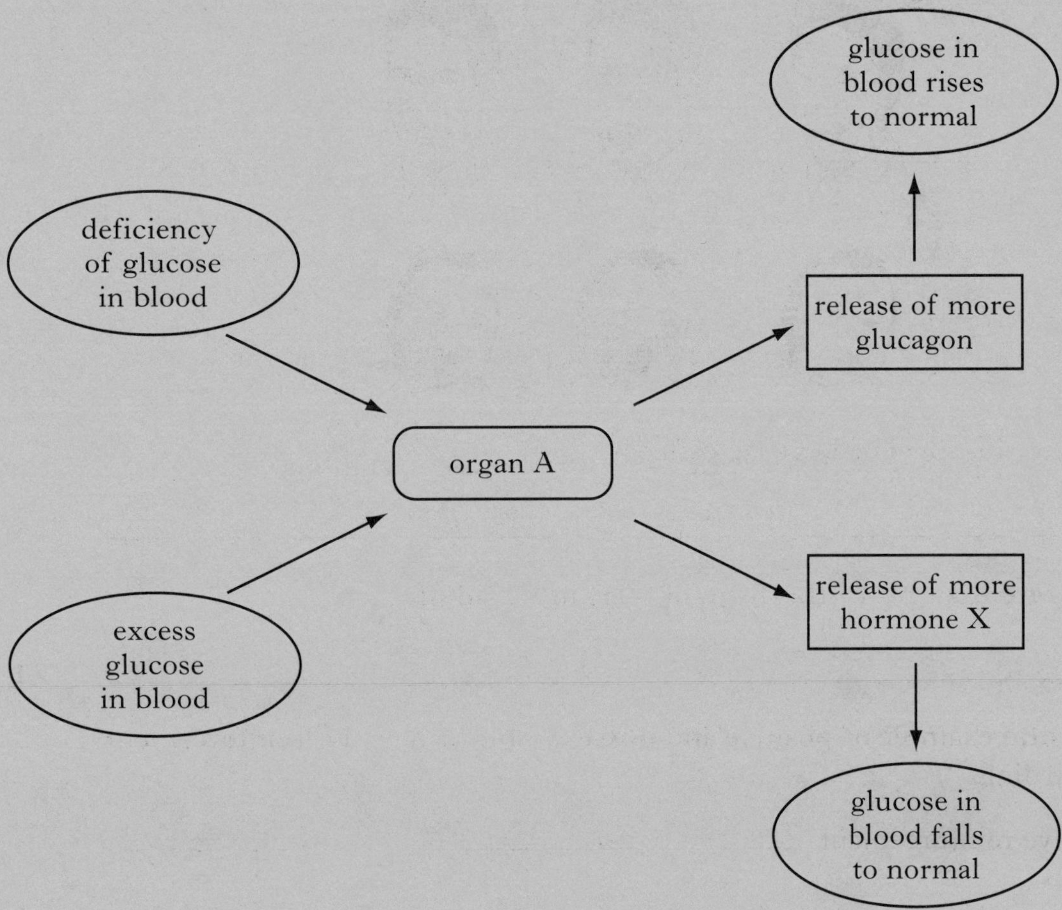

(*a*) Name organ A and the hormone X it produces.

OrganA ______________________________ 1

HormoneX ______________________________ 1

(*b*) (i) Glucose is stored as a carbohydrate. What is this carbohydrate called?

______________________________ 1

(ii) Give **one** important property of this carbohydrate

______________________________ 1

(*c*) Describe how glucose regulation illustrates negative feedback.

____

____

______________________________ 2

(*d*) Name another hormone produced in a stressful situation which can affect blood glucose levels.

______________________________ 1

DO NOT WRITE IN THIS MARGIN

MARKS

11. The diagram below shows a form of learning behaviour in human babies.

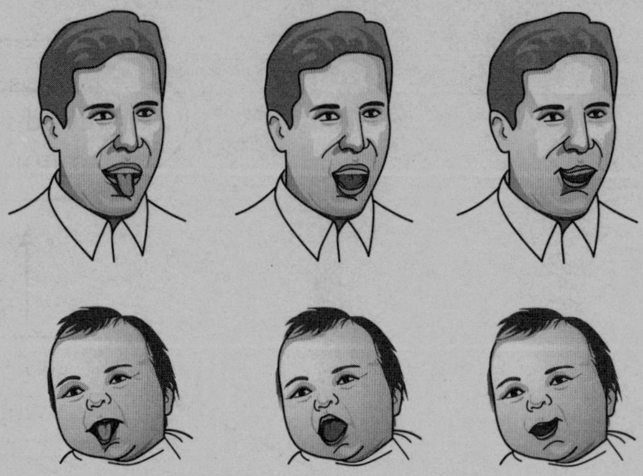

(*a*) What is this form of learning called?

_______________________________________ 1

(*b*) Give **one** example of this form of learning in adults.

_______________________________________ 1

(*c*) Give **one** example of positive and **one** example of negative reinforcement of learning.

Positive reinforcement _______________________

_______________________________________ 1

Negative reinforcement _______________________

_______________________________________ 1

(*d*) Behaviour is influenced by a combination of three important factors.

State these three factors and then explain **one** of them.

1 _______________________

2 _______________________

3 _______________________ 2

Factor _______________________

____

Explanation _______________________

____

_______________________________________ 1

DO NOT WRITE IN THIS MARGIN

MARKS

12. (*a*) Complete the following sentences by underlining one choice from each pair of words given in **bold**.

The sympathetic nervous system is part of the **central / autonomic** nervous system and can be found in the **cerebrum / medulla**. Sympathetic nerves **decrease / increase** sweating. 1

(*b*) What effect does the presence of a myelin sheath have on the function of a motor neurone?

____ 1

(*c*) The sympathetic and parasympathetic nervous systems often have opposite effects to each other.

What single word describes this? ____________________ 1

(*d*) Complete the following table which describes some of the parts of a sensory neurone.

Part	*Description*
	Carries information towards the central nervous system
Dendron	
	Where the cell nucleus is located

2

DO NOT WRITE IN THIS MARG

MARKS

13. It is estimated that for every 1% of our body mass we lose due to dehydration, our ability to do work goes down by approximately 10%.

The data below shows how loss in body mass due to dehydration affects ability to do work for a sample of males.

Loss in body mass (%)	*Ability to do work (%)*
0·0	100
1·0	95
2·0	90
3·0	80
4·0	75
5·0	65

(*a*) Draw a **line graph** of the data on the grid below.

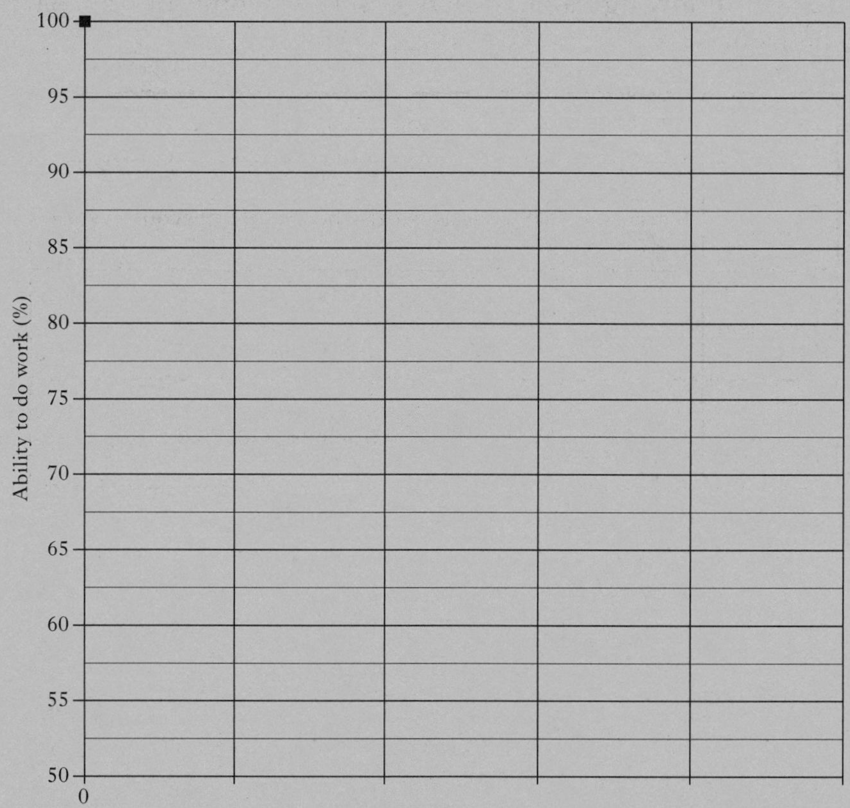

1

(*b*) Do the actual data support the estimate? Explain your answer.

Estimate supported by data ______________________________

Explanation ______________________________

______________________________ 1

(*c*) Give one way in which the actual data might be unreliable.

____

______________________________ 1

DO NOT WRITE IN THIS MARGIN

13. (continued)

MARKS

(*d*) A person weighs 70 kg and he is 75% water.

How much water will he have lost if his ability to do work has decreased by 10% and this is due to dehydration?

Space for calculation

________________ kg **2**

DO NOT WRITE IN THIS MARG

SECTION C

MARKS

Both questions in this section should be attempted.

Note that each question contains a choice.

Labelled diagrams may be used where appropriate.

1. Answer **either** A **or** B.

A. Write an account of the male reproductive system under the following headings:

(i) structure and function of the testes; **4**

(ii) contribution to fertilisation of the secretions of the prostate gland and seminal vesicles; **4**

(iii) adaptation of sperm for their function in reproduction. **2**

(10)

OR

B. Discuss memory under the following headings:

(i) encoding; **5**

(ii) storage. **5**

(10)

In question 2, ONE mark is available for coherence and ONE mark is available for relevance.

2. Answer **either** A **or** B.

A. Discuss the role of enzymes as catalysts in biochemical pathways. **(10)**

OR

B. Give an account of how blood pressure in vessels is caused and how it changes in different parts of the circulatory system. **(10)**

[End of question paper]

Exam 3

Leckie × Leckie
Scotland's leading educational publishers

Answer sheet for Section A:

Higher Human Biology
Practice Papers for SQA Exams

Please select your answer using a single mark e.g.

A	B	C	D
☐	■	☐	☐

	A	B	C	D
1.	☐	☐	☐	☐
2.	☐	☐	☐	☐
3.	☐	☐	☐	☐
4.	☐	☐	☐	☐
5.	☐	☐	☐	☐
6.	☐	☐	☐	☐
7.	☐	☐	☐	☐
8.	☐	☐	☐	☐
9.	☐	☐	☐	☐
10.	☐	☐	☐	☐
11.	☐	☐	☐	☐
12.	☐	☐	☐	☐
13.	☐	☐	☐	☐
14.	☐	☐	☐	☐
15.	☐	☐	☐	☐

	A	B	C	D
16.	☐	☐	☐	☐
17.	☐	☐	☐	☐
18.	☐	☐	☐	☐
19.	☐	☐	☐	☐
20.	☐	☐	☐	☐
21.	☐	☐	☐	☐
22.	☐	☐	☐	☐
23.	☐	☐	☐	☐
24.	☐	☐	☐	☐
25.	☐	☐	☐	☐
26.	☐	☐	☐	☐
27.	☐	☐	☐	☐
28.	☐	☐	☐	☐
29.	☐	☐	☐	☐
30.	☐	☐	☐	☐

Higher Human Biology

Practice Papers for SQA Exams

Time allowed: 1 hour 45 minutes

Exam 3

Fill in these boxes and read what is printed below.

Full name of school	Town
Forename(s)	**Surname**

Read each question carefully.

Attempt **all** questions.

Write your answers on the blank paper provided.

Write as neatly as possible.

Answer in sentences wherever possible.

Leckie × Leckie
Scotland's leading educational publishers

Read closely

1. For Section A, you should use an HB pencil and, where neccesary, a rubber.
2. Each Answer is **either** A, B, C or D. When you have decided your answer, use your pencil to put a line in the appropriate space on the answer sheet. (See the example below.)
3. Each question has **only one correct** answer.
4. Do not do any rough working on the answer sheet: use a separate sheet of paper.

Sample question

The surface area:volume ratio of a cube with edges 1 cm is

A 1:1

B 3:1

C 6:1

D 12:1

The correct answer is **C** – 6:1. This answer has been clearly marked in **pencil** below.

Changing an answer

If you need to change an answer, carefully rub out your original, then use your pencil to fill in the answer you now want. Below, the answer has been changed to **D**.

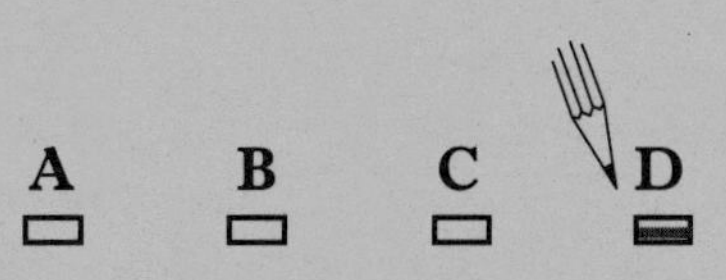

SECTION A

All questions in this section should be attempted.
Answers should be given on the separate answer sheet provided.

1. Which of the following would **not** be found in the matrix of a mitochondrion?

A Glucose

B Adenosine triphosphate

C Acetyl co-enzyme A

D Carbon dioxide.

2. Which of the following does **not** dissolve in water?

A Fructose

B Starch

C Glucose

D Maltose

3. The diagrams below show two types of mutation of a chromosome with the genes represented by letters.

A–B–C–D–E–F–G–H
[normal sequence of genes]

Mutation 1 A–B–D–E–F–G–H
Mutation 2 A–B–C–E–D–F–G–H

Which line in the table correctly names these two mutations?

	Mutation 1	*Mutation 2*
A	Deletion	Substitution
B	Insertion	Inversion
C	Deletion	Inversion
D	Inversion	Insertion

4. What will be the anticodon on the tRNA molecule for the DNA base triplet ACA?

A TGT

B ACA

C TCT

D UCU

5. The concentration of urea in a healthy person's urine was found to be 60 times as much as that found in the blood.

If a urine sample from such a person contained 6 g urea/litre, how much urea would be present in 100 cm^3 of blood?

A 1·0 g

B 0·1 g

C 0·01 g

D 0·001 g

6. Which of the following is **not** a role of proteins?

A Enzyme action

B Vitamin transport

C Muscle contraction

D Antibody formation

7. The following processes are involved in the production of the enzyme amylase in the mouth.

1 Translation of the mRNA by ribosomes in the cytoplasm

2 Transcription of the gene in the nucleus

3 mRNA leaves the nucleus

4 Amino acids joined by peptide bonds

5 Protein transported in endoplasmic reticulum

Which of the following is the correct sequence of these processes?

A 1→2→3→4→5

B 2→3→1→4→5

C 3→2→1→4→5

D 5→1→3→2→4

8. Meiosis ensures that

A the diploid number of chromosomes is maintained

B the gametes are diploid

C all the daughter cells are identical

D the quantity of DNA is the daughter cells is halved.

9. The diagram below shows the oxygen dissociation curves for two pigments (X) and (Y).

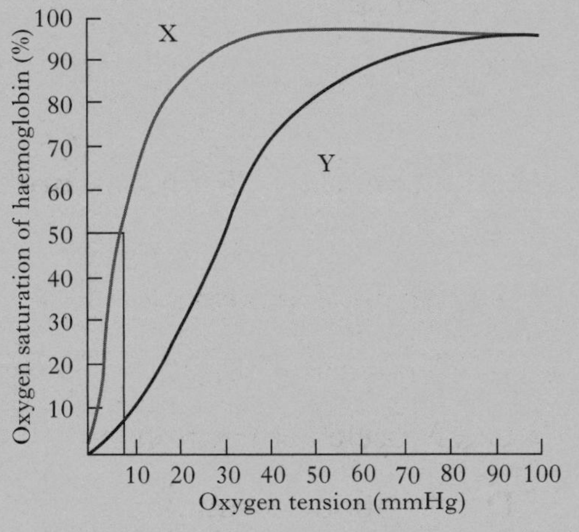

Tissues have low oxygen tension while lungs have high oxygen tension.

From the graph, it can be seen that X would be more effective than Y in transporting oxygen round the body because

A X can carry more oxygen than Y

B Y releases its oxygen more readily than X in the tissues

C at very high oxygen tensions, Y is more saturated than X

D Y is more saturated in the lungs than X

10. During the early months of pregnancy, progesterone is mainly produced in the

A *corpus luteum*

B pituitary

C interstitial cells

D placenta

11. If an egg is not fertilised, which of the following events does **not** take place?

A *Corpus luteum* breaks down.

B Menstruation.

C FSH levels fall.

D The egg secretes human chorionic gonadotrophin (HCG).

12. The diagram below shows two cubes (b) and (c), both made from combinations of cube (a).

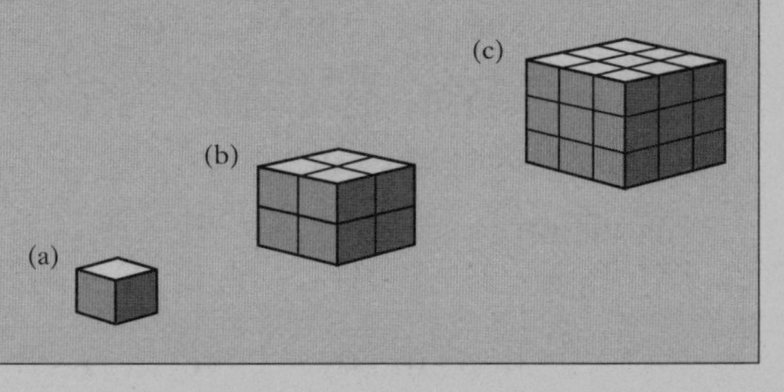

What is the surface area to volume ratio of structures (b) and (c)?

	Structure (b)	*Structure (c)*
A	3:1	2:1
B	6:1	4:1
C	2:1	3:1
D	2:3	3:4

13. The graph below shows the effect of increasing the concentration of a substrate on the rate of an enzyme-catalysed reaction.

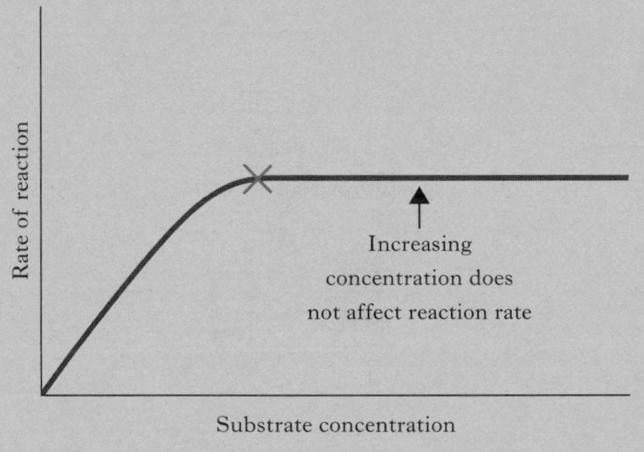

At point X

A adding more substrate will increase the rate of reaction

B the enzyme is no longer working

C enzyme inhibition has taken place

D some factor other than substrate concentration limiting the reaction rate.

14. Which line in the table describes some features of aerobic and anaerobic respiration are **true**?

	Aerobic respiration	*Anaerobic respiration*
A	*occurs in the cytoplasm*	*oxygen is used*
B	*forms pyruvic acid*	*lactic acid is formed*
C	*ATP is produced*	*occurs in the mitochondrial matrix*
D	*ATP is lost*	*needs NAD*

15. Which of the following causes an increase in the blood glucose levels?

A Antidiuretic hormone

B Oestrogen

C Insulin

D Glucagon

16. To prepare a 1% solution of vitamin C, solution from a 10% solution of vitamin C, it would be necessary to mix

A 5 cm^3 water with 10 cm^3 10% vitamin C solution

B 10 cm^3 water with 10 cm^3 10% vitamin C solution

C 50 cm^3 water with 10 cm^3 10% vitamin C solution

D 90 cm^3 water with 10 cm^3 10% vitamin C solution.

17. Puberty describes, amongst other changes, the start of the maturing of sexual organs.

From the graph below showing the growth of the sexual organs for a female, predict the age when this is likely to happen.

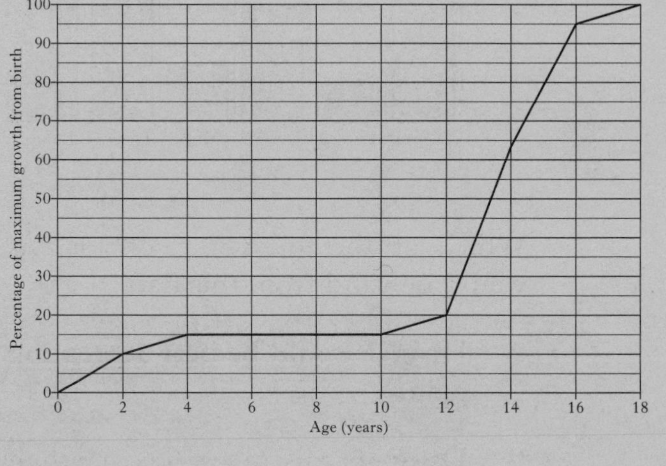

A 4 years

B 8 years

C 10 years

D 14 years

18. An experiment was carried out which looked at how long it took for six different drugs, used as painkillers, to dissolve in stomach acid.

The results are shown in the graph below.

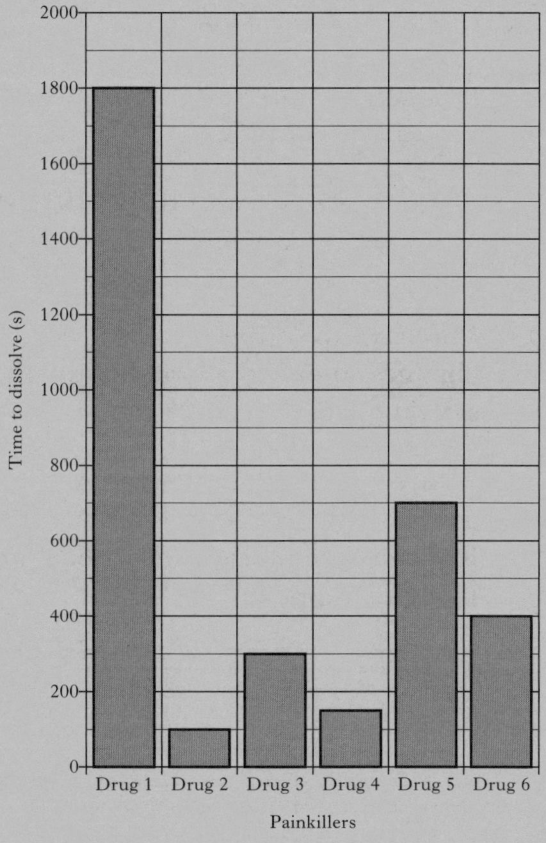

Which of the following conclusions would be valid from this data?

A Drug 2 would be best at treating pain.

B Drug 6 dissolves faster than drug 5.

C Painkillers do not dissolve well in water.

D Drug 2 takes the least time to dissolve.

19. The following diagram shows the structure of the population in Hong Kong in 2006.

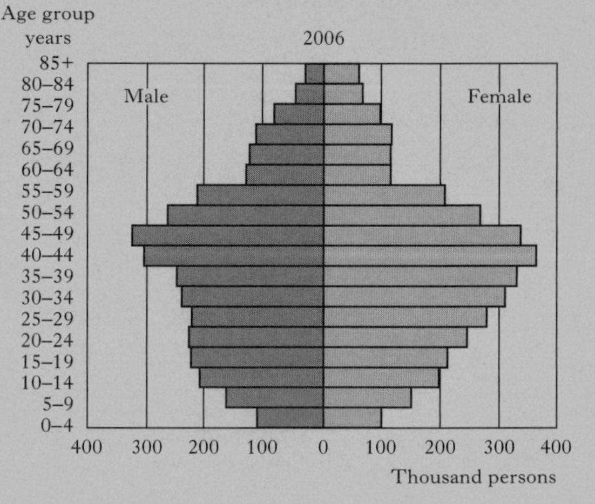

Which of the following conclusions is correct?

A The numbers of males and females over 85 years is the same.

B Most males are in the 45–49 years range.

C Most females in the population are younger than 20 years.

D Males tend to live longer than females.

20. Which of the following is **not** true? Blood pressure is high in the glomerulus because the

A blood vessel entering the glomerulus is wider than the one leaving

B renal artery is relatively near the heart

C resistance offered by the capillaries is great

D blood in the aorta is at a low pressure.

21. Albinism in humans is caused by a mutation of the gene involved in the production of the pigment melanin. The mutant allele is recessive and not sex-linked.

Two parents, who are normal for the production of the pigment, have an albino child.

Using A and a for the normal and mutant alleles respectively, what are the likely genotypes of the parents?

	Father	*Mother*
A	AA	Aa
B	Aa	AA
C	AA	AA
D	Aa	Aa

22. A person's environmental temperature rises. This is followed by a rise in his or her body temperature.

Which line of the table is the most likely combination of changes which will take place to restore the body temperature to normal?

	Sweating	*Blood vessels on skin*	*Hairs on skin*
A	increased	dilated	raised
B	increased	constricted	lowered
C	decreased	dilated	lowered
D	increased	dilated	lowered

23. Which of the following pairs of outcomes concerning selective breeding of crops is **not** beneficial to humans?

A Increased resistance to disease and being ready for cropping quicker

B Lower yield per unit area of land and improved nutritional content

C Resistance to drought conditions and easy to harvest

D Higher yield per unit area of land and increased sensitivity to changes in temperature

24. The graph below shows the changing heart beat, measured in beats per minute, for a person doing exercise for 6 minutes.

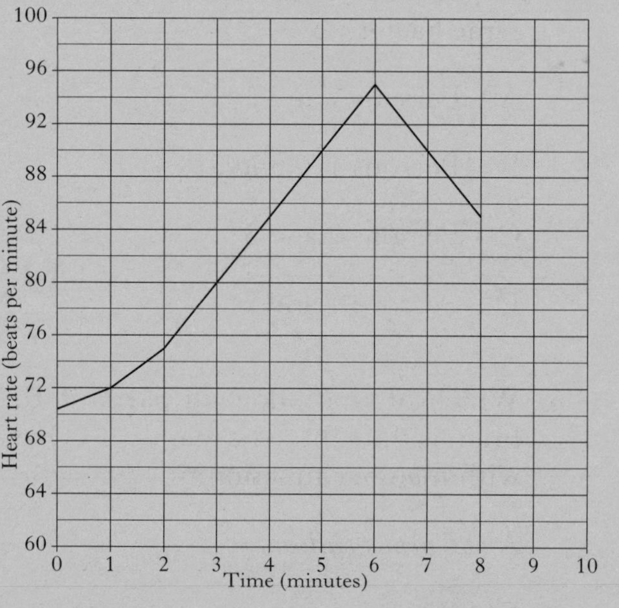

Assuming the rate of decrease in the heart rate remained the same, predict the likely heart rate (bpm) after 9 minutes.

A 80

B 78

C 76

D 75

25. The following three people encountered a bacterium which caused an infection in different ways.

Person 1 picked up the infection by inhaling contaminated water droplets in the air breathed out by an already infected person but made a full recovery with no medical intervention.

Person 2 was immunised against this bacterium beforehand and did not develop any symptoms on exposure to the contaminated water droplets.

Person 3 picked up the infection but was immediately put on the appropriate antibiotic drug to kill the bacterium and made a full recovery.

25. (continued)

Which of these people would be able to make a "secondary immune response" to a further exposure to the same bacterium?

A Persons 1 and 3

B Persons 1, 2 and 3

C Persons 2 and 3

D Persons 1 and 2

26. Which of the following parts of the brain is thought to be mainly involved with memory function?

A *Corpus callosum*

B Pituitary

C Limbic system

D Medulla

27. A student was out with a group of friends and decided it was time to leave. The friends pressed the student to stay even though he wanted to leave and so he stayed.

This is an example of

A social facilitation

B deindividuation

C internalisation

D peer pressure.

28. Which line in the table correctly describes the function of prostaglandins and testosterone?

	Prostaglandins	*Testosterone*
A	stimulate uterine muscle to contract	cause testes to produce sperm
B	cause testes to produce sperm	provide nourishment for sperm
C	provide energy source for sperm	stimulate uterine muscle to contract
D	develops secondary sexual characteristics	reduces pH of semen

29. Which of the following descriptions of growth hormone is **not** true?

A It is produced by the pituitary gland.

B It stimulates growth of the skeleton.

C It is under the control of a gene for its production.

D It is secreted by the hypothalamus.

30. Which of the following is a response by the immune system?

A Production of antigens in response to an infection

B B-cells secreting antigens

C T-cells phagocytosing antibodies

D B-lymphocytes producing antibodies

DO NOT WRITE IN THIS MARGIN

SECTION B

All questions in this section should be attempted.

MARKS

1. The diagram below shows the structure of an organelle involved in the production of an enzyme.

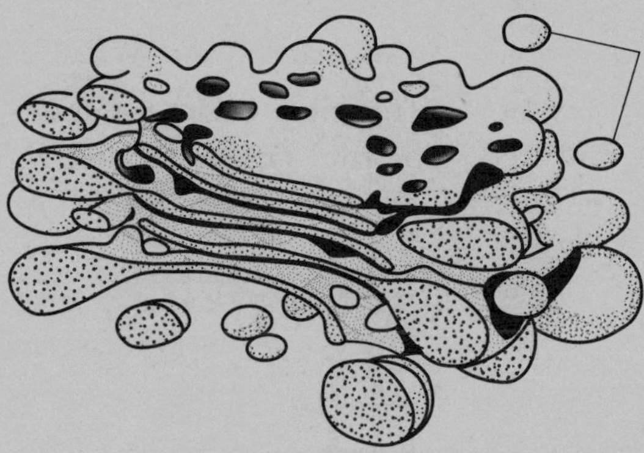

(*a*) Name the structure shown and briefly state its function.

Structure ______________________________

Function ______________________________

______________________________ 2

(*b*) Why would this organelle be found in large numbers in salivary glands?

____

______________________________ 1

(*c*) Some of the secretory vesicles can go on to be lysosomes.

Give **one** function of lysosomes.

______________________________ 1

(*d*) Give an example of a cell which would contain many lysosomes.

______________________________ 1

(*e*) What term is used for the process by which cells take in tiny volumes of extracellular fluids, and enclose these in vesicles?

______________________________ 1

MARKS

2. Patients with an infection in their lungs produce a great deal of mucus which may inhibit the effectiveness of an antibiotic.

A group of 50 patients with similar lung infections was divided into two groups. One group was treated with an antibiotic alone, while the other received the same antibiotic plus an additional drug which helped to break up mucus and so allow the antibiotic to be more effective.

Samples of mucus were collected every hour after the treatment was started and the concentration of antibiotic analysed. The higher the concentration of antibiotic in the sample, the more effective it is at treating the infection.

The results are shown below:

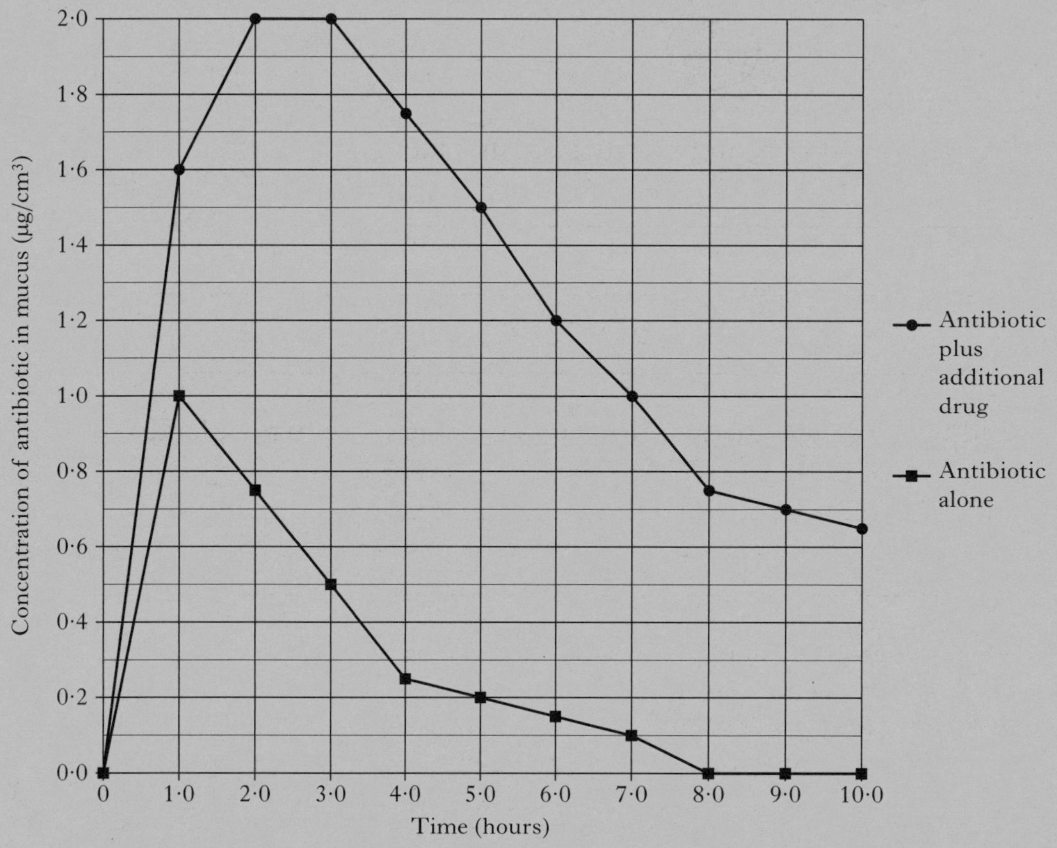

(*a*) How long does it take for the concentration of the antibiotic in the presence of the additional drug to be four times that of the antibiotic alone in a mucus sample?

________________________ hours **1**

(*b*) Give **two** differences in the results with and without the additional drug.

1 ____

____

2 ____

____ **2**

DO NOT WRITE IN THIS MARGIN

MARKS

2. (continued)

(*c*) State **two** design features of this investigation which would make the results unreliable.

1 ______________________________

____

2 ______________________________

______________________________ **2**

(*d*) Based only on the data given, what conclusion can be made?

____

______________________________ **1**

3. The following diagram shows how an enzyme E can be prevented from acting on its normal substrate S by an inhibitor I.

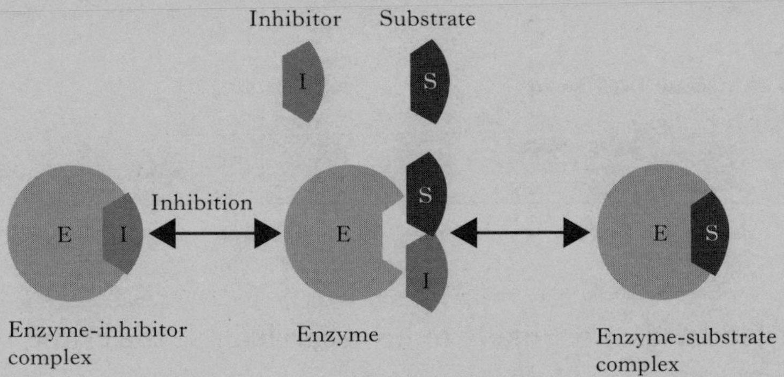

(*a*) What type of inhibition is shown here? Give a reason for your answer.

Type: ______________________________

Reason: ______________________________

____

______________________________ **2**

(*b*) What effect would increasing the concentration of the substrate have on the inhibitor's ability to slow down the enzyme-catalysed reaction? Give a reason for your answer.

Effect: ______________________________

____

Reason: ______________________________

______________________________ **2**

3. (continued)

MARKS

(*c*) Name an enzyme which cyanide can inhibit.

____

______________________________ **1**

4. (*a*) Three individuals, P1, P2 and P3, were suspected of a crime. A sample of blood fluid from each was compared with a sample of body fluid taken from the crime scene and genetic fingerprints were produced.

The diagram below shows the results.

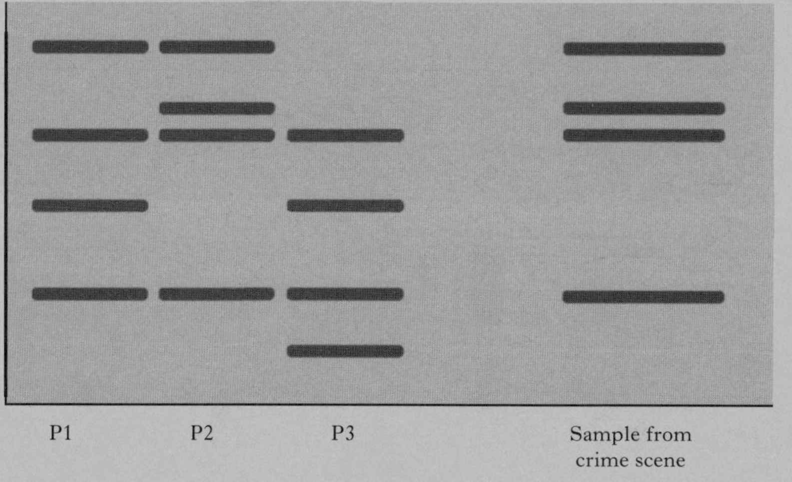

Which of the individuals is most likely to have carried out the crime? Give a reason for your answer.

Individual ______________

Reason ______________________________

______________________________ **2**

(*b*) Each band on a person's genetic fingerprint must match one in the father's genetic fingerprint or one in the mother's genetic fingerprint.

Explain why this is the case.

____

______________________________ **1**

(*c*) Give **one** example, other than solving crime, of how genetic fingerprinting can be used.

______________________________ **1**

DO NOT WRITE IN THIS MARGIN

4. (continued)

MARKS

(*d*) Women have XX sex chromosomes while men have XY sex chromosomes.

Which of the following grandparents must be the source of genes on a man's Y-chromosome?

Underline your answer then give a reason.

Father's mother   Mother's father   Father's father

Reason ______________________________

______________________________ **2**

(*e*) What term is used to describe chromosomes other than sex-chromosomes?

______________________________ **1**

5. (*a*) The following diagram shows how the levels of testosterone in the blood are controlled.

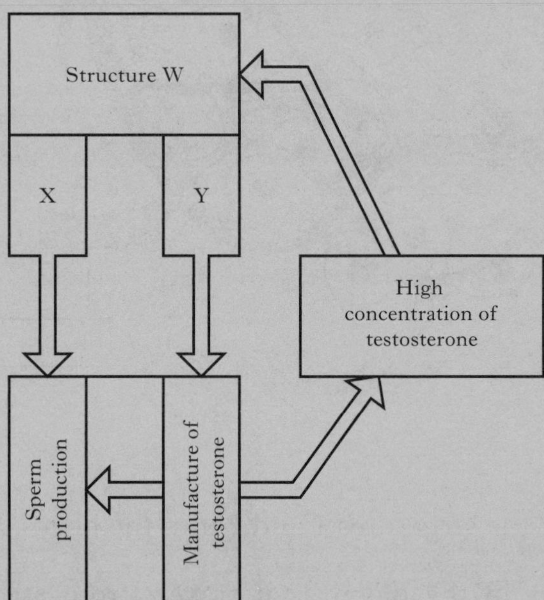

(i) Identify Structure W: ______________________________ **1**

(ii) Which hormones are represented by the letters X and Y?

X ______________________________

Y ______________________________ **1**

(iii) What is the effect of high concentrations of testosterone on structure W?

____

______________________________ **1**

DO NOT WRITE IN THIS MARGIN

5. (continued)

MARKS

(*b*) Give **one** example of a cause of male infertility and state how it might be treated.

Cause ______________________________

Treatment ______________________________ **2**

(*c*) What function does the hormone oxytocin perform in the birth process?

____

______________________________ **1**

6. The diagram below shows part of a capillary network.

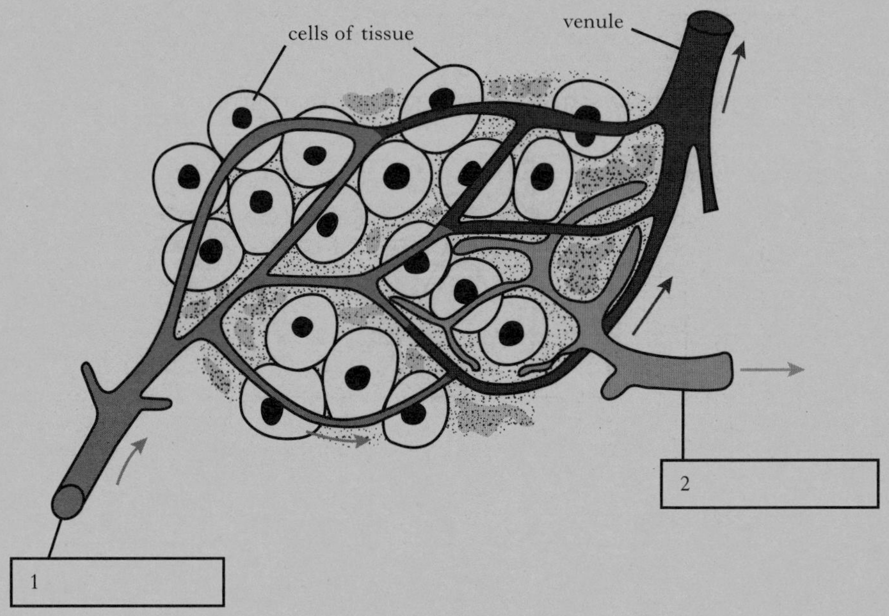

(*a*) Insert the names of the structures 1 and 2 into the boxes provided. **1**

(*b*) Give **TWO** changes in the blood as it travels from structure 1 to the venule.

1 ______________________________

2 ______________________________ **2**

(*c*) Indicate, by means of an arrow the direction of flow of the fluid in structure 2. **1**

(*d*) Name the fluid found in structure 2. ______________________________ **1**

(*e*) Which type of molecule is not likely to be found in structure 2? Give a reason for your answer.

Molecule: ______________________________

Reason ______________________________

______________________________ **2**

DO NOT WRITE IN THIS MARGIN

MARKS

7. (*a*) The graph below shows the changes in performance of female reproductive systems and maximum heart rates over time.

The results are based on how well women perform compared to when they are 20 years of age, expressed as a percentage.

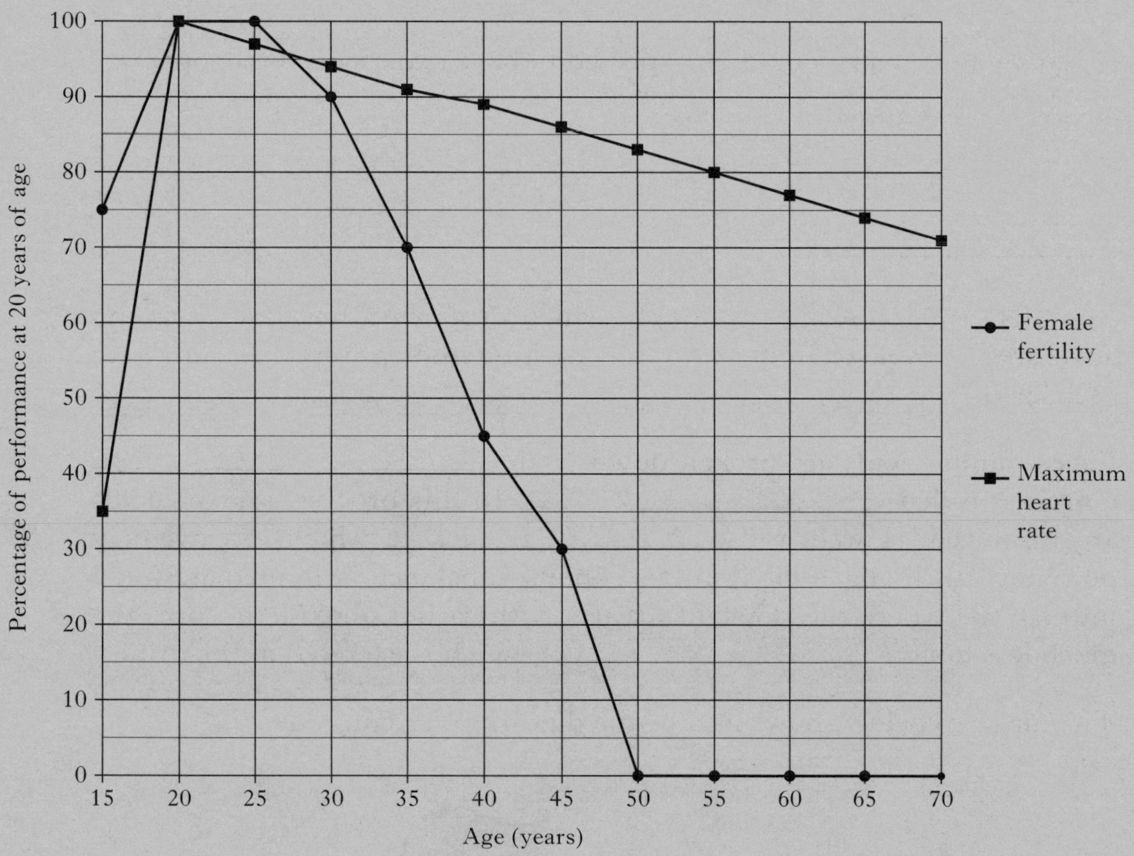

(i) State **TWO** conclusions which can be drawn from these results.

1 ______________________________

____

2 ______________________________

______________________________ **2**

(ii) Assuming the rate of change for the maximum heart rate stays the same, predict the maximum heart rate for an 80 year old female as a percentage of what it was when she was 20 years old.

______________________________ % **1**

(iii) Between which two ages is the greatest change in female fertility?

______________________ and ______________________ years **1**

(iv) For how long do women have 100% fertility?

______________________ years **1**

DO NOT WRITE IN THIS MARGIN

7. (continued)

MARKS

(*b*) It is estimated that about 8% of women experience menopause by the age of 40 years.

In a population of 200 women, 25% of them were found to be 40 years or older.

Calculate how many would be expected to have experienced menopause.

Space for calculation

____________________ **1**

8. (*a*) Complete the following paragraph, which deals with how excess amino acids are metabolised in the body, by inserting **one** appropriate word in to each space.

Excess amino acids are broken down in the ____________________ in a process called ____________________. In this process, organic acids are produced as well as ____________________ which is extremely poisonous to living cells. This poisonous substance is immediately fed into a cycle where the substance reacts with carbon dioxide to form the much less toxic ____________________ which is excreted in the urine. **3**

(*b*) The diagram below shows part of the digestive system.

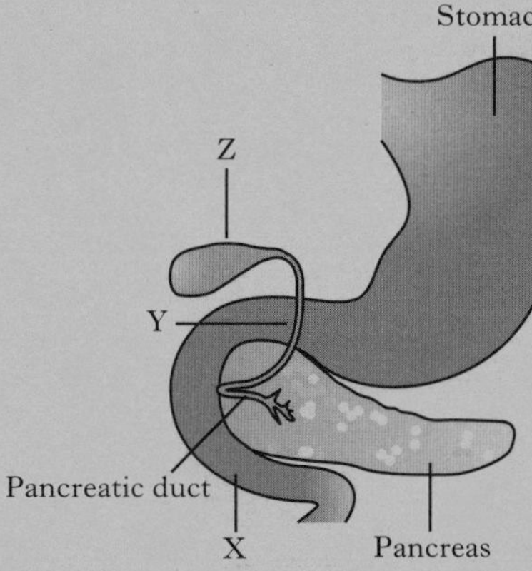

(i) Identify structures X, Y and Z.

X ____

Y ____

Z ____ **3**

(ii) Name the substance stored in structure Z. Give **one** function of this substance.

Substance ____________________

Function ____

____ **2**

DO NOT WRITE IN THIS MARGIN

MARKS

9. The following diagram shows some of the stages involved in regulating the level of glucose in the blood.

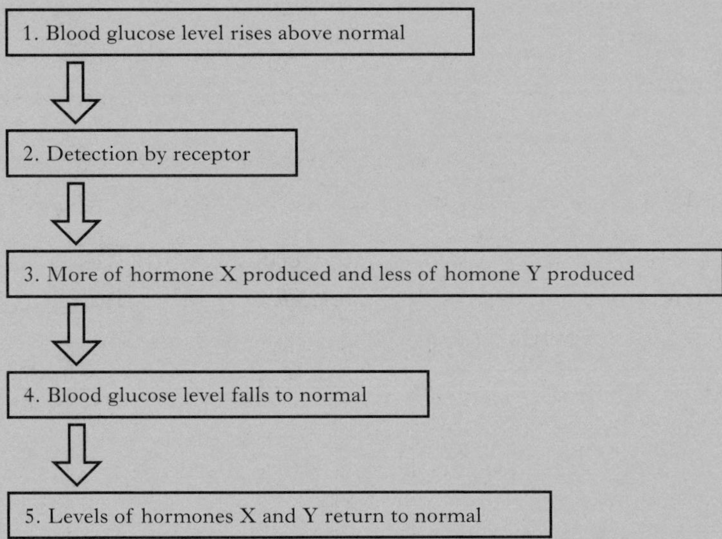

(*a*) Where is the receptor for detecting blood glucose levels located?

____ **1**

(*b*) Names hormones X and Y.

X ____________________

Y ____________________ **2**

(*c*) Explain how the regulation of glucose levels demonstrates negative feedback.

____

____

____ **2**

(*d*) (i) What is the main stimulus which causes the breathing rate to increase?

____ **1**

(ii) Where in the brain is the respiratory control centre?

____ **1**

DO NOT WRITE IN THIS MARGIN

MARKS

10. The graph below shows how quickly people react to a stimulus, measured in milliseconds (ms), depending on whether they have taken a caffeine drink before the task.

100 people were randomly divided into two groups. Both groups were asked not to take any caffeinated drink for 24 hours before the experiment.

One group was given a caffeine drink while the other was given a drink which was identical except it had no caffeine.

Each person was given 5 trials, each of which consisted of 50 measurements of their reaction time. All the results, for each person and then for the whole group, were averaged as shown.

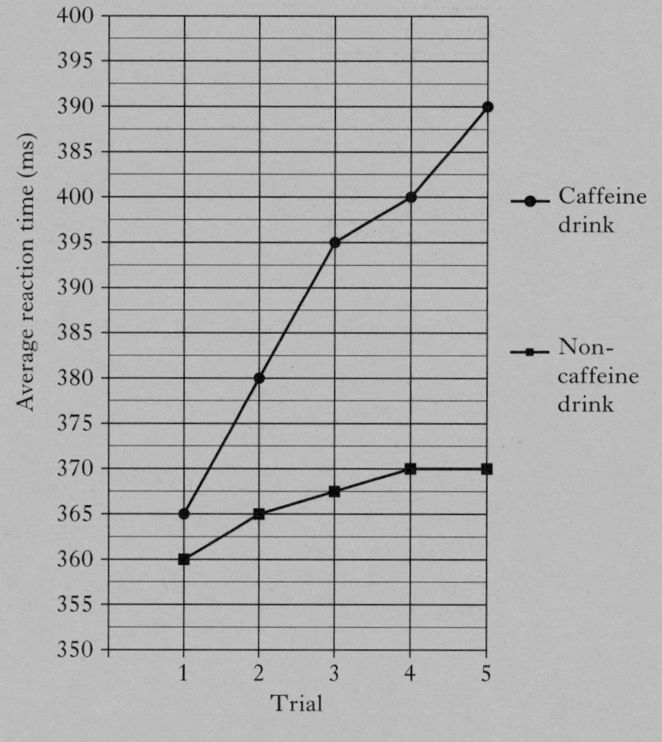

(*a*) The experimenter claimed that drinking caffeine lowered reaction time.

Give **two** reasons why this conclusion might not be correct.

1 ______________________________

____

2 ______________________________

______________________________ **2**

(*b*) State **two** ways in which the validity of this experimental procedure could be improved.

1 ______________________________

____

2 ______________________________

______________________________ **2**

DO NOT WRITE IN THIS MARGIN

MARKS

11. The diagram below shows the junction between two nerve endings.

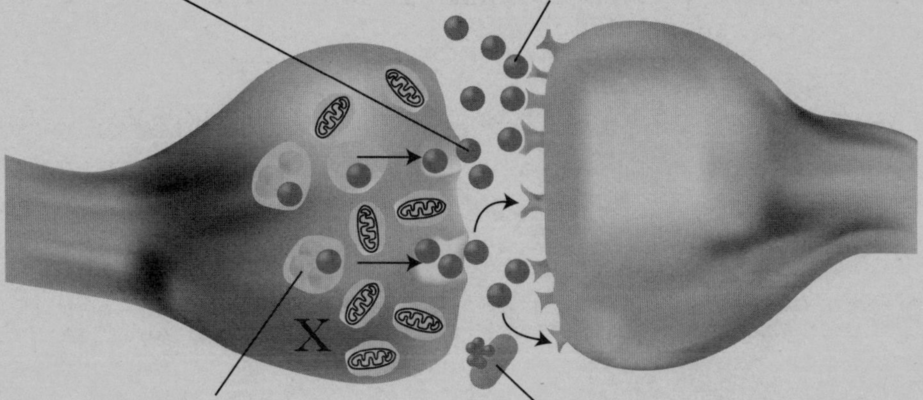

(*a*) Name this type of junction.

______________________________ 1

(*b*) In each box below the diagram, state the type of fibre involved. 2

(*c*) Give **one** example of a neurotransmitter and state what would trigger its release.

Example: ______________________________

Trigger: ______________________________ 2

(*d*) Give **two** reasons why these junctions are important.

1 ______________________________

____

2 ______________________________

______________________________ 2

(*e*) Why would mitochondria be present in large numbers at X?

____

____

______________________________ 2

DO NOT WRITE IN THIS MARGIN

MARKS

12. The following experiment relates to the activity of two enzymes, X and Y, on the egg protein albumin at five different pHs.

The diagram shows how cores of solid egg white were removed from boiled eggs.

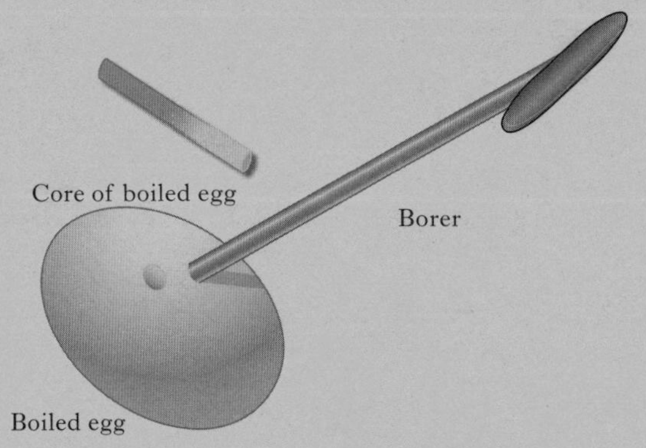

Five cores, all 30 mm long, were placed in a solution of enzyme X at pH 4·0 and five were placed in a solution of enzyme Y at pH 4·0.

This was repeated at pH values of 5·0, 6·0, 7·0 and 8·0

After 45 minutes, the lengths of the five cores in each enzyme in the different pHs were measured and the individual results and averages are shown in **Table 1.**

Table 1 Lengths of cores (mm) after 45 minutes.

Enzyme X						*Enzyme Y*					
Core	*pH*					*Core*	*pH*				
	4·0	*5·0*	*6·0*	*7·0*	*8·0*		*4·0*	*5·0*	*6·0*	*7·0*	*8·0*
1	15·1	21·9	29·5	28·8	30·0	*1*	30·0	29·7	24·0	22·1	16·0
2	15·5	19·8	29·0	29·9	29·8	*2*	29·9	28·9	24·8	21·9	15·9
3	14·8	19·9	28·6	29·6	29·8	*3*	29·7	29·7	23·9	22·2	15·8
4	14·9	21·9	28·8	29·5	29·9	*4*	30·0	29·7	24·1	21·6	16·1
5	15·2	20·0	28·6	29·7	30·0	*5*	29·9	30·0	23·7	21·7	15·7
Ave	15·1	20·7		29·5		*Ave*	29·9		24·1	21·9	15·9

(*a*) Complete **Table 1** by calculating the missing averages lengths **1**

Space for calculation

DO NOT WRITE IN THIS MARGIN

12. (continued)

MARKS

(*b*) Draw **line graphs** for the averages from **Table 1**.

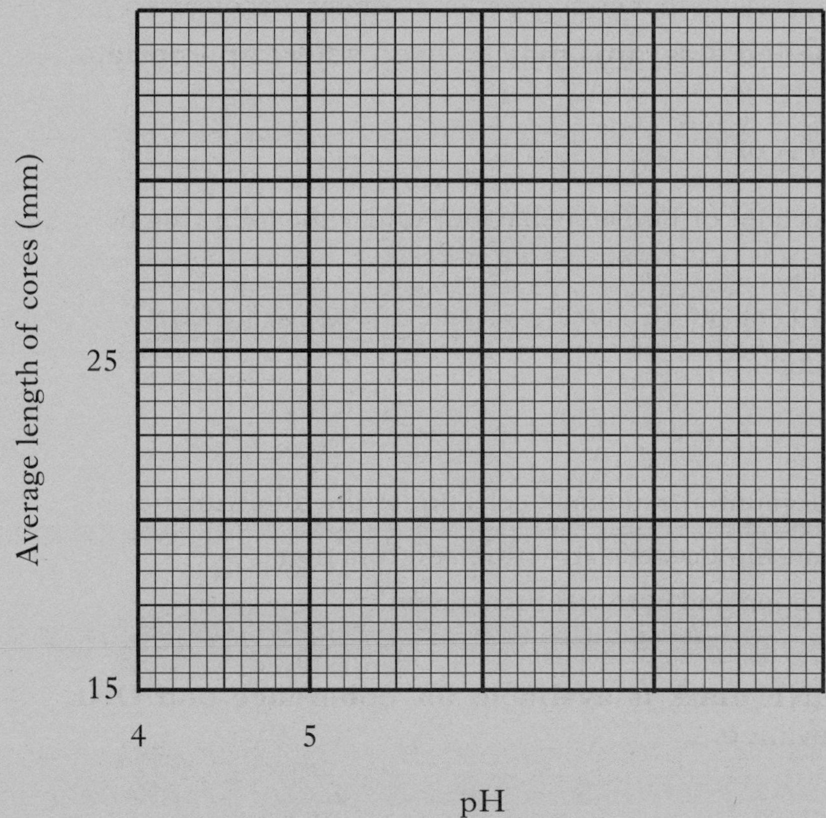

3

(*c*) Give **one** valid conclusion suggested by the data for each enzyme. 2

Enzyme X ______________________________

____

Enzyme Y ______________________________

____

(*d*) State **one** assumption which was made about each of the cores at the start of the experiment. 1

____

(*e*) State **two** design flaws in this experimental procedure. 2

1 ______________________________

____

2 ______________________________

____

SECTION C

MARKS

Both questions in this section should be attempted.

Note that each question contains a choice.

Labelled diagrams may be used where appropriate.

1. Answer **either** A **or** B.

A. Give an account of human behaviour under the following headings:

(i) shaping; **3**

(ii) reinforcement; **4**

(iii) extinction. **4**

(10)

OR

B. Write an account of red blood cells under the following headings:

(i) relationship between structure and function; **4**

(ii) production and eventual breakdown. **6**

(10)

In question 2, ONE mark is available for coherence and ONE mark is available for relevance.

2. Answer **either** A **or** B.

A. Describe the structure of the plasma membrane and explain how it functions in action transport. **(10)**

OR

B. How do aerobic and anaerobic respiration in human cells differ? **(10)**

[End of question paper]

Worked Answers

Answers to Practice Exam 1

SECTION A

1. D PS

> *HINT*
>
> Remember the complementary base pairs are C – G and T – A so if there are 60 cytosine bases there must be 60 guanine bases. This leaves 130 bases split equally between thymine and adenine 65:65 each. The percentage of thymine must be $(65 \div 250) \times 100$.

2. D KU

> *HINT*
>
> Enteropeptidase activates trypsinogen to form trypsin.
>
> Most vitamins can act as co-enzymes.
>
> A co-factor is a non-protein substance.
>
> The specificity of an enzyme is dependent on the molecular structure of the active site into which the specific substrate will fit so D is correct here.

3. A KU

> *HINT*
>
> You are expected to know the "many roles of lipids within the body to include energy store, heat and nerve insulation, fat pads on feet and hands, vitamin transport and hormones." Fats, by their very nature, act as stores or reserves of energy and as such, are not readily metabolised for energy. Only when carbohydrate reserves are depleted are fats then metabolised.

4. A KU

> *HINT*
>
> Here you have to remember that human viruses are composed mainly of nucleic acid (DNA or RNA) and protein. Notice you don't actually have to know that swine flu (H1N1) virus specifically contains RNA but you can deduce the correct answer provided you know the basic structure of human viruses.

5. A PS

> *HINT*
>
> By adding an equal volume of water to an equal volume of the stock solution, the technician is effectively diluting it by a factor of 2 from 1·8% to 0·9% which is what is required.

6. B PS

> *HINT*
>
> This is a straight-forward question which just requires you to work through each possible answer in turn.
>
> Lactose is both soluble and does not react with Clinistix so A is true.
>
> Fructose is soluble and does react with Barfoed's so B is not true.
>
> Glucose is soluble and does react with Clinistix so C is true.
>
> Only starch is insoluble so D is true.
>
> Note that if you are confident about a statement being false, there is no need to work through the others. Alternatively, if you are unsure then by eliminating the true ones, you can deduce the false statement.

7. D KU

> *HINT*
>
> The hormones involved in human reproduction are varied and complex in their interaction. You would do well to construct good diagrams to help you remember their names and how they influence each other.

8. D KU

> *HINT*
>
> It is important to understand the mechanism by which identical (monozygotic) and non-identical (dizygotic) twins arise. In identical twins, only one egg is fertilised by only one sperm and the zygote, after it starts to divide, somehow separates to become two genetically identical cells (a clone in fact) which go on to develop as two identical twins. However, in non-identical twins, two ova are fertilised by two different sperm making the babies as unlike as any two siblings, of different sex for example.

9. B KU

HINT Terms can often be confusing when they sound or look similar. Think of uterus, ureter and urethra for example! Chromatids are the individual identical strands which are held in pairs by centromeres before the meiosis process starts. As such, the two strands make up one chromosome and it is the chromosomes during the first stage of meiosis, not the chromatids, which are separated. Each member of a homologous pair of chromosomes is pulled to opposite poles of the cell.

10. A PS

HINT This is a simple arithmetical calculation.

Each minute after exercise, the girl breaths 30 times and each breath has a volume 1200 cm^3. This gives a volume of 30 x 1200 = 36,000 cm^3 per minute, of which 15 percent is oxygen giving a volume of oxygen (15 x 36,000) ÷ 100 = 5400 cm^3.

Remember that the time asked is 5 minutes so you have to multiply this by 5 giving in total

5 x 5400 = 27,000 cm^3

Expressed in litres, this is 27 litres.

11. B KU

HINT This is a simple question on the basic functions of the brain parts. Higher activities, such as thought processing, are carried out in the cerebral hemispheres.

12. C KU

HINT The topic of the nervous system is riddled with terms which can be difficult. You really need to learn these, perhaps by using flash cards. When you have, this question is easy!

13. C PS

HINT To answer this question, you need to find two points on the graph where the trace starts to repeat itself. You can choose, for example, time 0 s and time 0·8 s or the two peaks. The gap will be 0·8 s which gives a calculated value for the heart rate of (10 x 60) ÷ 8 = 75 beats per minute.

14. D KU

HINT In general, the sympathetic nervous systems speeds up body processes but there are sometimes exceptions. For example, the sympathetic nervous system slows down peristalsis while the parasympathetic speeds this up. Learning this lends itself well to constructing a table similar to the one in this question.

15. C KU

HINT This is a very basic question on hormones.

16. B PS

HINT You need to check each statement here.

After 30 minutes John's blood glucose level was 140 mg/100 cm^3 which is not twice his original value of 85 mg/100 cm^3 so A is incorrect.

James's blood glucose level dropped from 165 to 100 = 65 mg/100 cm^3 which represents a percentage drop of (65 ÷ 165) x 100 = 39% which is very close to the value of 40% making B correct.

After 60 minutes James's blood glucose level was 10 mg/100 cm^3 higher than John's which represents a percentage of (10 ÷ 90) x 100 = 11% not 20% so C is incorrect.

John returned to his base level of 85 mg/100 cm^3 within 90 minutes whereas James was still higher than his original after the same time so D is incorrect.

17. C KU

HINT

With all genetics questions, no matter how obvious you think the answer is, you should take time to draw a Punnett square to check your answer. One of these is shown below for the correct answer but you should routinely do this for all possible.

Gametes	X^B	X^b
X^b	X^BX^b	X^bX^b
Y	X^BY	X^bY

This is the only combination, from the options given, which would make it possible for this couple to have an affected daughter and an unaffected son.

18. D KU

HINT

Births and immigrations both increase the population size while deaths and emigrations decrease it.

19. C KU

HINT

Only photosynthesis has the net effect of removing carbon dioxide from the atmosphere.

20. C KU

HINT

Rehearsing something helps transfer it to long-term memory.

21. B PS

HINT

You simply have to look at the values for each of the two age bands, 50–54 and 55–59 to work out the total percentage as 3 + 2·5 = 5·5%.

22. C KU

HINT

Here the boy has developed a fear of all snakes based on his experience with one. This is called generalisation: the ability to respond to related stimuli in the same way.

23. B KU

HINT

Since monozygotic twins are genetically identical, the effect of their genes has less impact on their development than how they are raised, that is, their environment. If such a pair was raised separately, then the effect of the environment would be the predominant factor affecting their development. Such situations do occur rarely but of course it would be unethical to carry out such an investigation deliberately.

24. A PS

HINT

When a gene is knocked out of normal action by a mutation, the enzyme it produces will not work on its specific substrate properly. This means the substrate is not changed into its product(s).

A mutation in G1 would stop E1 from working and so X could not be converted into Y and would therefore accumulate. A is the correct answer.

A mutation in G1 would not affect the proper working of E2 so Y would be metabolised into Z and would not gather. B is therefore wrong.

A mutation in G2 would stop E2 being synthesised. C is therefore wrong.

A mutation in G2 would not stop the next enzyme in turn from acting on Z which would decrease. D is therefore wrong.

25. C PS

HINT

Generally, practising improves performance for most human activities. You need to be careful not to make any conclusions which are not supported the evidence.

The improvement was not uniform over the trial period since the graph is not linear so A is wrong.

The time taken to perform the task does seem to decrease the time taken so B is wrong.

Most improvement was shown at the early stages with the first 10 or so trials, after which time the improvement starts to level out, so C is correct.

You cannot extrapolate (go further) here with the data since you don't actually know what would happen with further trials so D is wrong.

26. D PS

HINT

This is a question testing your ability to "plan, design and evaluate experimental procedures". It could well be that you have carried out this actual experiment, but this need not be the case to answer these questions.

The action of ATP could be the result of it being an enzyme. Since enzymes are proteins, boiling the ATP should prevent it working but in fact it would not thus proving it can't be an enzyme. A would therefore improve the design of this experiment.

Repeating experiments is almost always sound scientific procedure and helps to validate the results so B is another strategy for improving experimental design.

Controls are needed all the time in biological experiments. They help prove what is the actual cause of a change.

Using a different sugar solution would make no difference to the design of the experiment. This would just be the same experimental design but on a different sugar!

27. C KU

HINT

Ideally there would be no need to use chemicals to control pests but realistically this is not the case. Growers therefore strive to use the minimum quantity to control the pest but to minimise potential damage to the host crop and other non-target organisms (plants and animals) are not affected. Of the options given, C is the best.

28. C KU

HINT

There are a number of factors which together, in sequence, will cause desertification. This question is an over-simplification but nevertheless the order of events is accurate.

29. D KU

30. A KU

SECTION B

1. (*a*)

Letter	*Name*	*Function*
A	mitochondrion	provides ATP
B	secretory vesicle	transport materials out of the cell
D	rough endoplasmic reticulum	protein synthesis

[3] KU

HINT: Make sure you use the full description for D as "rough" endoplasmic reticulum.

One mark is awarded for each correctly completed row. Remember there are no half-marks in the National Paper!

(*b*) (i) One of the five nuclear pores labelled. [1] KU

HINT: Make sure the line ends exactly on the structure you intend to indicate and do not use arrow-heads.

(ii) Allow large and/or insoluble molecules to pass into and out from the nucleus. [1] KU

HINT: You could also answer this by giving an example such as "allows mRNA to leave the nucleus".

(*c*) Presents a large surface area. [1] KU

HINT: The idea of the importance of surface area is found widely in Biology. Think of the lungs, the shape of a red blood cell or the lining of the intestine.

2. (*a*)

Ile	*Ile*	*Leu*	*Gln*	*Glu*	*Leu*	*Glu*	*Glu*	*Glu*	*Leu*

[2] PS

HINT: At first sight this seems quite a daunting question but in fact, if you break it down, it is quite straightforward. Complete the missing "Ile" first using up all the "AUA" codons of which there are two. Now complete the missing "Glu" using up all the "GAG" codons of which there are four. The codon "CAA" appears only once and therefore must be Gln leaving the other three spaces for Leu.

To obtain both marks, all eight amino acids must be correct with six or seven correct obtaining one mark.

(*b*) UAU GUU GAA [1] PS

HINT: The anti-codon in each case will be the complementary base triplet to the mRNA codon. If you have made an error in part (a) of this question but give the correct complementary base triplet, there will be no additional penalty. In other words, the error from one question is not carried to the next related one.

(*c*) mRNA is single-stranded while DNA is double-stranded/mRNA contains uracil instead of thymine present in DNA/mRNA contains ribose DNA contains deoxyribose. [1] KU

HINT: Any two of these differences would obtain the mark but there are no half marks for partial answers. Also, be careful to complete the comparison in each case. For example, "mRNA is single-stranded" is not enough.

(*d*) $30 \div 45 = 0{\cdot}67$ seconds [1] PS

3. (*a*) [1] PS

Plant source	*Average*
Potato	0·9
Leek	3·7
Parsnip	6·7
Radish	0·35

(*b*) [2] PS

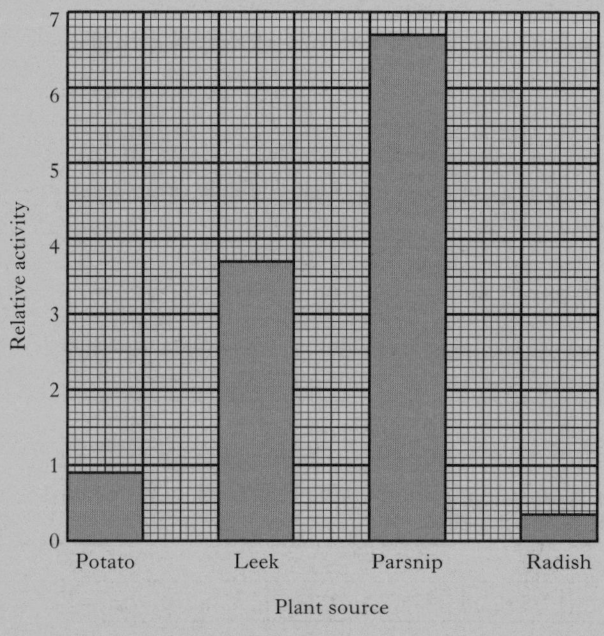

HINT

Remember, when constructing bar charts, always label each axis correctly and include units where appropriate. This is a very common source of loss of marks for students. Also, separate each bar by the same spacing, make each bar has the same width, use more than 50% of the grid and draw each bar with a ruler very carefully. Notice the use of bold type to draw your attention to a particular instruction, here to draw a bar chart using the average results.

One mark for labelling each axis correctly and one mark for correct plotting of the data.

(*c*) (i) By repeating the experiment [1] PS

HINT

Carrying out an experiment only twice does not generate results which are particularly reliable.

(ii) Constant temperature/same time in blender/same method of measuring volumes of oxygen given off [1] PS

HINT

In any experiment, it is important to control all the variables **except** the one you are investigating. Here that variable is the different plant sources so it is important to keep all the other variables constant. Some have been considered by the student. The variables above are some possible answers.

(iii) Use boiled plant tissue/material/repeat with distilled water instead of H_2O_2 [1] PS

HINT

Catalase is an enzyme: a common control for enzyme experiments, to prove enzyme function, is to boil the enzyme/enzyme source to denature the protein structure of the enzyme.

4.

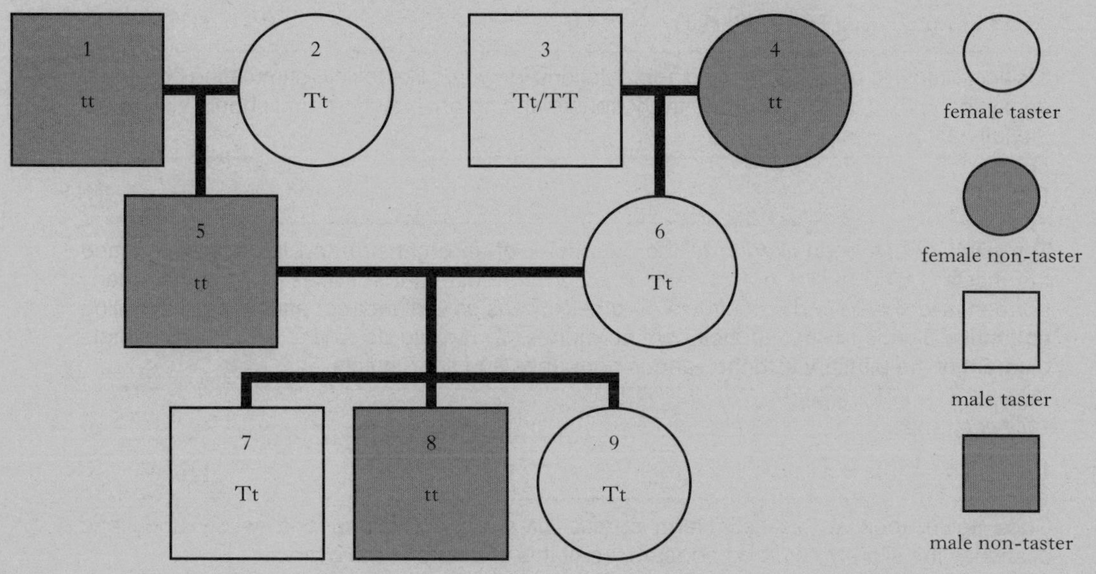

(*a*) (i) 1 tt 6 Tt [1] PS

> **HINT** The easiest way to tackle this question is to fill in, on the diagram, the genotypes of the people you know for sure who are non-tasters. They must be tt and are individual 1, 4, 5 and 8. Next, you can work out the genotypes of individuals 2, 6, 7 and 9 who all must be heterozygotes since they can taste but either have children who are non-tasters or parents who are non-tasters. This leaves individual 3 whose daughter, individual 6, is a taster. Individual 3 can be either TT or Tt and without further information, we cannot decide for sure.

(ii) 4 [1] PS

(iii) 3 [1] PS

This man could be either TT or Tt and still have a daughter (individual 6) who is a taster since his partner is tt. [1] PS

(*b*) When two or more genes are responsible for controlling an inherited characteristic/trait.

[1] KU

> **HINT** It is important to appreciate that the simple Mendelian type genetics learned in the course are not the complete description of inheritance. This is complex and varied and one example is the situation where inherited differences, such as intelligence and height, are controlled by more than one gene.

5. (*a*) (i) 8 [1] KU

> **HINT** Students often confuse chromosome and chromatid. Chromatids can be considered as half of a duplicated chromosome. Each one of a pair of chromatids, joined by a centromere, is identical to the other. During cell division, when chromatids are separated, they are then termed chromosomes. In cell A, there are four chromosomes shown, each one of which consists of two identical chromatids, making eight in all.

(ii) Spindle/spindle apparatus/spindle fibre

Pulls chromatids apart/separates chromatids [2] KU

(iii) A

Whole chromosomes are being pulled apart. [2] KU

(*b*) Diploid [1] KU

> **HINT** Since the daughter cells will all contain the same genetic material as the original parent cell B, they are termed diploid. Do not confuse this with haploid, the term used to describe the genetic complement of daughter cells which arise from meiosis, as would be the case for cell A.

(*c*) Gonads/testes/ovaries [1] KU

6. (*a*) (i) Ovulation [1] KU

(ii) A rise in Luteinising Hormone (LH) [1] KU

> **HINT** It is acceptable to use the standard abbreviations for words like follicle-stimulating hormone, deoxyribonucleic acid, adenosine triphosphate and so on. However, you should also know the full name of each.

(iii) Pituitary [1] KU

> **HINT** The pituitary has been likened to the conductor of an orchestra and is often nicknamed the master gland because it co-ordinates so many different activities. It produces many hormones which have direct effects on other organs as well indirect effects by stimulating endocrine glands to secrete their own hormones. You would do well to construct a simple diagram of the pituitary with the various hormones and their effects.

(iv) *Corpus luteum*

Progesterone and oestrogen [2] KU

> **HINT** Once again, look at this Latin term *corpus luteum*. It literally means yellow body and describes the slightly coloured appearance of this structure in the ovary.
>
> Both hormones are needed for the mark here.

(v) X should indicate the wall of the uterus [1] KU

> **HINT** You need to be careful when labelling diagrams to ensure you indicate exactly the structure you intend. Here, you are not asked to use a line, though that would be acceptable. Instead, you should insert the letter X exactly on the wall of the uterus which is where a normal implantation would take place.

(*b*) During *in vitro* fertilisation, eggs and sperm are allowed to mix outside the body of the female.

One of the fertilised eggs/zygotes is then placed/implanted in the wall of the uterus. [2] KU

> **HINT** *In vitro* literally means *in glass* and is an apt description of how this process is artificial, outwith the female's body. It is often useful to have an understanding of Latin terms used in biology, rather than learning by rote.
>
> Both points are needed here to obtain the two marks.

7. (*a*) (i) P should be inside the left ventricle (bottom right hand chamber on page). [1] KU

> **HINT** The structure of the heart and the associated structures are best learned visually, using well labelled diagrams. Use arrows to indicate the flow of the blood.

(ii) A Sinoatrial node B Atrioventricular node [2] KU

(iii) Sends out electrical impulses to ensure both atria contract at the same time. [1] KU

> **HINT** Make sure you are aware of the function of both the sinoatrial and atrioventricular nodes and the interplay between them.

(*b*) Diastole [1] KU

> **HINT** Make sure you understand the distinction between systole and diastole.

8. (*a*) Even with no exposure to radiation, there are always some random mutations occurring naturally.

[1] KU

> **HINT** It is important to appreciate that all humans carry, to a greater or lesser extent, naturally occurring mutations, even without any exposure to a mutation-causing agent such as radiation.

(*b*) 4·0–5·0 hours [1] PS

> **HINT** You simply have to read the graph to work out the increase in the number of mutations for each of the ranges given for type A. For 4·0–5·0 hours, it is 20 per person which is higher than all the others.

8. (continued)

(*c*) 2·5–3·00 hours [1] PS

> HINT: Notice the question specifies the block of time as 30 minutes so you need to look at each such block separately and note the increase. For example between 2·00 and 2·5 hours the increase was from 25 to 40 mutations per person.

(*d*) (i) Type B [1] PS

(ii) At exposure times upto 3·5 hours, type B causes more mutations than type A/Type A only causes mutations after 3·5 hours' exposure whereas type B starts to cause mutations after 0·5 hours' exposure. [2] PS

> HINT: There are a variety of ways of answering this question but be careful to give two different reasons, not two which say the same thing. In the first answer given above, only one of these would be acceptable and you would need to supply another different one such as suggested here.

(*e*) (i) Insertion and substitution. [2] KU

> HINT: Make sure you understand the different types of gene mutation, insertion, deletion, substitution and inversion.

(ii) Insertion

Since an extra nucleotide pair has been inserted, the whole sequence of bases after this mutation is altered.

AND

The protein/sequence of amino acids coded for by the changed mRNA will be different from that point onwards. [2] KU

> HINT: You must get both reasons correct to obtain both the marks here.

9. (*a*) Arteriole A, venule C, lymph vessel B [1] KU

> HINT: You can deduce from the diagram the blood is moving from A into C. Therefore in A it is away from the heart. Such blood vessels are called arteries and the smaller examples of these arterioles. C is a venule taking blood back to the heart.

(*b*) X excess tissue fluid is being absorbed into the lymph vessel

Y tissue fluid is being reabsorbed back into the blood capillary [2] KU

> HINT: You need to understand that as fluid leaks under pressure from arterioles, it is mostly reabsorbed back into the surrounding capillaries to be returned to the heart. However, the system does not reabsorb all the leaked fluid and the excess is then taken up by the lymph system as shown here. Notice the importance of the term "excess" in this answer.

(*c*) Capillaries are so narrow, there is frictional resistance as the blood moves through which causes a drop in pressure. [1] KU

(*d*) Diffusion [1] KU

> HINT: A simple one-word answer here to describe this process which occurs widely, for example, in the lungs to allow for gaseous exchange.

(*e*) To prevent the backflow of lymph/stop lymph flowing backwards. [1] KU

> HINT: Anywhere that valves are present, think of preventing the backflow of some fluid such as blood or, as here, lymph.

10. (*a*) In 1990 the greatest percentage of smokers were in the 24–27 group whereas in 2000 the greatest percentage of smokers were in the 20–23 group.

In both 1990 and 2000, the smallest percentage of smokers were in the same 16–19 group.

In 1990 the percentage of smokers rose for each age group but in 2000, the percentage of smokers rose from ages 16–23 then fell for 24–27. [2] PS

> *HINT* You can expect one larger data-handling type question in the National Examination worth around 7 or 8 marks. Usually this question will have more than one set of data represented in different ways such as tables, pie-charts, line-graphs and so on. Take your time with this question and work steadily through each question only after studying the data first. You may need to read over this several times.
>
> Any two points here for the two marks.

(*b*) 8 : 3 [1] PS

> *HINT* Remember to reduce the ratio to the simplest whole number. Do not write 40:15. Also, in your answer preserve the order of the question. In this case, 1990 should come first.

(*c*) This group may have been more likely to have read about the dangers of smoking/more likely to be educated about the risks of smoking/family background less liable to contain smokers. [1] PS

> *HINT* There is no single answer to this question and any reasonable answer, such as the examples given, will obtain the mark.

(*d*) 440 [1] PS

> *HINT* First, work out the percentage of manual workers by subtracting the total of the other two groups from 100 to give 55%. Remember the question gave the sample size of the people in 2008 as 1000. 55% of this is 550 and of these, 80% are men.

(*e*) Sample size is not indicated for the age groups/no account taken of sex of people for either representation/limited to a particular geographical area/only 2 years' data shown/1000 is too small a sample/different types of cigarettes may be smoked. [2] PS

> *HINT* Again here, a number of possible answers would be accepted. A few examples are given and any two such answers would get both marks.

(*f*) Could allow agencies to forward-plan services/target specific age groups/spend more money according to socio-economic groups. [1] PS

> *HINT* A variety of possible answers would get the mark here. Some of these are shown.

11. (*a*) Central nervous system [1] KU

> *HINT* The nervous system in humans is very complex and is best learned using diagrams and flow charts. Flash cards are an ideal way of reinforcing the learning of the terms.

(*b*) Autonomic system. [1] KU

> *HINT* This controls activities below the level of consciousness such as breathing, digestion, heart beat and so forth.

(*c*) Motor nerve cells/motor neurone [1] KU

(*d*) Receptor → dendrites → cell body → axon → effector [2] KU

> *HINT* All five correct for 2 marks. Three correct for 1 mark.

(*e*) $2{\cdot}8 \div 120 = 0{\cdot}023$ seconds [1] PS

> *HINT* This is a very theoretical question in that the speed of nerve transmission varies enormously throughout the body. However, it is essentially a simple arithmetic calculation.

12. (*a*) Joins the two cerebral hemispheres together/acts as a bridge between the two halves of the cerebrum transfers information between hemispheres [1] KU

(*b*) (i) Paw [1] PS

HINT: This is a difficult question on split-brain function. When the corpus callosum is cut, the two hemispheres can't communicate with each other properly and so, while the person perceives both images, he or she only "speak" the image of the paw which the left hemisphere has seen because that is also where the speech centre is located.

(ii) Bowl of cereal [1] PS

HINT: Here, the person's right hemisphere has "seen" the bowl of cereal. He or she can't speak the words because the right hemisphere does not have language function but he or she can indicate what he saw with his left hand whose function is controlled by the right hemisphere.

13. (*a*) Nitrate/fertiliser/phosphate/potassium/pesticide [1] KU

HINT: You cannot use the word fertiliser here since it is already given in the diagram.

(*b*) Increased rainfall [1] KU

HINT: This would cause the fertiliser to be washed out of the soil into the drains and then into the stream.

(*c*) Eutrophication/algal bloom [1] KU

(*d*) When algae die, bacteria which break them down multiply.

The aerobic respiration of the bacteria uses up the oxygen in the water.

Fish which depend on dissolved oxygen die. [2] KU

HINT: All of these points would be needed to obtain full marks. Always take note of the weighting given to a question. This is worth two marks so requires a fuller treatment than a one mark question.

SECTION C

1. A (i)

- At the start of the marathon, athletes will use up glucose released from glycogen stores in muscles
- These stores are used for muscle action but supply is quickly used up
- Glucose is made available to the muscles via the bloodstream from liver glycogen
- Runner needs to have both carbohydrate and fat
- Which one is the dominant energy source depends on how much of each is available
- The body next adapts to fat metabolism
- Fatty acids are broken down to release energy in the later stages of the marathon
- In the liver, fatty acids are converted to acetyl-CoA which provides energy via the Krebs cycle

Any 5 of these

(ii)

- Starvation can be defined as serious loss of nutrients, preventing maintenance of good health
- Period of starvation must be prolonged before body starts to use protein
- Initially the body uses up its glycogen stores
- After this stage the body makes use of its fat stores
- Eventually the body utilises body protein
- Such as that found in muscle of the skeleton and heart
- Can lead to permanent organ damage or even death

Any 5 of these

1. B (i)

- Allergies are extreme sensitivities of the body's defence system to certain harmless antigens
- Allergic reactions are very rapid and sensitive to even minute quantities of the antigen
- Typical antigens are pollen, animal hair and fluff
- Reactions can occur in the nasal and bronchial passages as well as in the gastrointestinal tract and skin
- Antibodies are produced which bind to certain cells causing the release of histamine
- Histamine causes an inflammatory response
- This inflammatory response causes smooth muscle to contract
- Blood vessels dilate and become leaky
- Histamine is also responsible for the symptoms of sneezing/itchiness of the skin/watering of the eyes

Any 6 of these

(ii)

- In autoimmune diseases, immune reactions develop against components of body cells
- Rheumatoid arthritis may occur due to an immune response against the cells in the joints resulting in inflammation
- Juvenile diabetes is caused by an immune response against cells of the pancreas
- Viruses, drugs or genetic mutations may alter the surface antigens of some cells enough to cause them to be recognised as foreign
- Multiple sclerosis is another example of an autoimmune disease
- The body's own immune system attacks the myelin sheath of certain nerve cells

Any 4 of these

2. A

- Mechanisms attempt to maintain core temperature at a normal value of 37 °C
- In order to maintain a constant temperature in the structures below the skin, the heat produced must balance the heat lost
- Damage to tissues will result from overheating which is fatal because of protein denaturation
- Too low an internal temperature is fatal because the heart beat becomes irregular
- Mechanisms may be voluntary such as putting on/taking off extra clothing, increased/decreased activity, taking hot/cold drinks, raising/lowering temperature of the environment, looking for shelter/going into open air, curling up/spreading arms and legs to reduce/increase exposed surface area (any two of these for raising temperature and any two for lowering temperature)

2. A (continued)

- Mechanisms may be involuntary such as causing peripheral blood vessels in the skin to constrict/dilate to stop/encourage loss of heat, raising/lowering the rate of metabolism to generate more/less heat, shivering to make muscles produce heat in cold, hairs on skin becoming erect to improve insulation in cold, decreased/increased sweating (any two of these for raising temperature and any two for lowering temperature)
- The internal temperature hardly fluctuates more than 1°C from the normal value
- The main temperature regulatory centre of involuntary control is in the hypothalamus
- Hypothalamus receives information from temperature receptors located in the skin and the hypothalamus itself
- Hypothalamus responds to changes in the blood temperature
- These involuntary responses stimulate lowering of body temperature
- If the temperature falls below normal, involuntary responses raise body temperature
- Hypothalamus effectively acts as a body thermostat

2. B

- Estimated that the burning of fossil fuels is adding carbon dioxide to the atmosphere at the rate of some 2·3 parts per million per year
- Most of the increased carbon dioxide production is absorbed by dissolving in ocean waters which act as a sink but this sink is not unlimited
- Some increased carbon dioxide is used up by increased photosynthetic activity
- Not all the extra carbon dioxide can be absorbed which has a unbalancing effect on the equilibrium of the carbon cycles
- The natural land and sea carbon cycles can cope with most but not all of this additional loading
- Concern is that the increasing carbon dioxide levels could cause the onset of increased global warming
- Causing polar ice caps to melt/sea levels to rise/flooding of rivers/changing weather patterns (any two of these)
- Carbon dioxide allows solar shortwave radiation to pass through easily but absorbs longwave radiation reflected back from the earth's surface
- A rise in the temperature of the lower atmosphere otherwise known as the greenhouse effect
- A similar effect is caused by other carbon compounds such as carbon monoxide from car exhaust fumes/chlorofluorocarbons (CFC gases)/methane which is a natural product of decomposition and gas production from farm animals (any one from these)
- Present knowledge of global meteorology cannot allow accurate predictions of the effects of global warming
- Supports the view that continued damaging of the natural carbon cycle should actively be discouraged

Answers to Practice Exam 2

SECTION A

1. B KU

HINT A very strong indication of the correct answer is given by the label "ribosomes." This suggests a rough surface which is indeed true of the rough endoplasmic reticulum.

2. B KU

HINT Actin and myosin are the contractile proteins involved in muscle action. Remember, muscles can only pull, not push, and to do this, the actin and myosin proteins slide into one another, shortening (contracting) the biceps muscle.

3. D KU

HINT There are several ways in which materials can enter and leave a cell which involve passage across the cell membrane. Endocytosis and exocytosis both involve such movement and phagocytosis is a specific example of endocytosis, the taking into a cell across the membrane of substances in small membrane-bound sacs called vesicles.

4. A KU

HINT All of these substances, except starch, have nitrogen in their chemical structures. Glucagon, you remember, is a hormone which regulates blood sugar level and is a protein.

5. B PS

HINT Do not be put off by this table which looks a little complicated. It is typical of data used to show trends over a period of time and to make comparisons between different groups, here males and females.

Survival rates for men with cancer of the oesophagus have increased from 12% to 22%, an overall increase of 10%. For stomach cancer, the increase has been from 13% to 25%, an overall increase of 12% (which is greater than that of cancer of the oesophagus) so A is true.

Over the whole period, comparing women with men for survival of stomach cancer, women have always fared better so B is false.

In the period 1986–1990, 48% of people (males and females together) survived cancer of the oesophagus whereas 52% of people (males and females together) survived stomach cancer so C is true.

During the periods 1976–1980 and 1981–1985, in men the survival rate increased from 14% to 20%, an overall increase of 6% which was the greatest increase so D is true.

6. D PS

HINT Osmosis is a special case of diffusion of water through a semi-permeable membrane from an area of high water concentration to an area of low water concentration (i.e. down a concentration gradient). Once you have this concept firmly understood, you should be confident tackling this type of question. Only the water molecules are small enough to pass through the pores of the semi-permeable membrane. Sucrose molecules are too large so water will diffuse from A to B, lowering the level in A and raising it in B. Sucrose will remain trapped in tube B.

7. D PS

HINT

Notice the father is unaffected and the mother is a carrier. If the allele for this condition was dominant the mother could not be a carrier, whether or not the condition was sex-linked. We can conclude therefore the allele must be recessive. The father is unaffected and therefore must have two recessive alleles while the mother must be heterozygous since she is free from any symptoms but is a carrier. By studying the pattern of behaviour in their four children, it is possible to see the condition must be sex-linked since they have an affected son who would have two dominant disease-causing alleles, which is not possible because we already know that the disease-causing allele is recessive. Remember, the affected son inherits one of each form of allele from each parent. To be affected his father would have to be able to pass on one defective allele. We can be sure, therefore, the condition is both sex-linked and caused by a recessive allele.

8. A KU

HINT

The functions of the testes are to produce both the hormone testosterone and the sperm themselves. These two functions are carried out by the interstitial cells and seminiferous tubules respectively.

9. A KU

10. A KU

HINT

Remember that arteries carry blood away from the heart and veins towards the heart. Vessel 1 is leaving the heart and must be an artery as is vessel 3. For the same reason, vessels 2 and 4 must be veins since they are returning blood towards the heart. Providing you remember this, you can usually work out answers, even if you can't always remember actual names!

11. C KU

12. B KU

HINT

This can be quite a confusing section of the course. It's best to consider whether the person is making his/her own antibodies. If so, then this is an active immunity and if not, it is a passive immunity. Next, consider whether the exposure to the antigen is natural, for example, by breathing in a cold virus, or is artificial, for example, by receiving an immunisation.

13 B PS

HINT

Add the two figures together to get 0·6 seconds. This is the time for one heart beat. To obtain the number of beats in one minute you need to carry out this calculation

$(10 \times 60) \div 6 = 100$

14. D KU

HINT

In answering questions related to blood donation, always remember to match the donor's red blood cell antigen, A or B, with the recipient's plasma, which may contain various combinations of antibodies A and B. Thus a donor whose blood group is A must not give blood to someone whose plasma contains anti-A. Such a person could be blood group B or O. Once you have practiced this rule and mastered it, you will find these questions much easier to handle.

15. C KU

HINT

As a human grows, the surface of the body does not grow in proportion to the volume. You can try working this out using a number of similar-sized small boxes. As you double the box size by putting one on top of the other, two inner surfaces get lost. In other words, the smaller the box, the greater proportionally is the surface area compared to its volume. The same is true of humans. Small babies are at great risk from cold environments precisely because they lose heat so quickly from a relatively large surface area compared to their volume.

16. D PS

HINT The best way to tackle this question is to see that if, within the age group 6–11 months, 12% did not survive, that means that 100 – 12 = 88% did survive. 88% of 1300 is 1144.

17. D PS

HINT Within the age group 0–5 months, 15% of the babies did not survive. 15% of 500 is 75.

18. A KU

HINT The nitrogen cycle is essentially Standard Grade work but questions can occasionally be asked because of the linkage with the effects of excess nitrogen on the environment. You should revise this topic and make sure you are familiar with the elements of this complicated process. A diagram is almost always the best way to learn something like this.

19. B KU

HINT A key point in this question is the use of the phrase "…to drop quickly." This is because the oxygen is used up by bacteria, which multiply every 20 minutes in response to the increased nutrient level supplied by the untreated sewage. As they multiply and respire, the oxygen level in the river falls rapidly.

20. C PS

HINT As we get older, our ability to regulate our body temperature becomes less efficient. An older person also has a much larger surface area to volume ratio. These two variables combined, cause an older person to be at much greater risk of hypothermia than a younger person.

21. D PS

HINT From 120 to 150 minutes, the 18 year old's body temperature dropped from 36·4 °C to 36·0 °C, a drop of 0·4 °C. If this continued over the next 30 minutes, his new temperature would be 36·0 – 0·4 = 35·6 °C.

22. C KU

23. A KU

HINT Do not confuse the terms used in the section on behaviour. Flash cards would be a very good way of learning and distinguishing between the terms used.

24. D KU

HINT Humans need to be able to change their responses to stimuli which are similar but not the same. For example, not all red fruit is necessarily good to eat! See advice for question 23.

25. D PS

HINT At age 10–12 the recommended intake is 2200 and this increases to 2600 for a male aged 13–15 years. This is an increase of 400 calories which is (400÷2200) x 100 = 18% (rounded down).

26. C PS

HINT Notice the bold text which asks for this answer to be expressed as the simplest whole number ratio. While A is the ratio of the recommended values, it is not the simplest form. Each of these can be divided by 50 to reduce the larger numbers to the smaller whole numbers given in C.

27. B KU

HINT While all of these processes can be useful in helping us to remember things (and revising for examinations!), the particular technique used was to go over and over the same information until it passed from his short-term into his long-term memory.

28. D KU

HINT

After neurotransmitters have completed their function at a synapse, they have to be removed in some way. Two important ways are reabsorption and enzymatic breakdown. Noradrenaline is an example of a neurotransmitter which is reabsorbed while acetylcholine is broken down by an enzyme (acetylcholinesterase).

29. D KU

HINT

Patients who have split brains, usually caused by surgically cutting the *corpus callosum*, do not necessarily have impaired memory function. This procedure is anatomical/physical rather than molecular so does not support the molecular theory of memory.

30. A KU

HINT

RNA cannot have thymine which is replaced by the base uracil. Also, the sugar in RNA is ribose, not deoxyribose.

SECTION B

1. (*a*) The enzyme needed to convert phenylalanine to tyrosine is missing/not made. [1] KU

(*b*) The mother produces the enzyme necessary to convert phenylalanine to tyrosine. [1] KU

(*c*) The baby is put on a diet which is low in phenylalanine. [1] KU

(*d*) (i) Inborn error of metabolism [1] KU

(ii) Albinism [1] KU

(*e*) Neo natal testing/post-natal/newborn testing. [1] KU

(*f*) (i) Liver [1] KU

(ii) Deamination [1] KU

2. (*a*) [2] KU

Blood group	*Antigens present on surface of red blood cells*	*Antibodies present in the plasma*
A	antigen A	antibody B
B	antigen B	antibody A
AB	both antigens A and B	neither antibody
O	neither antigen	antibody A and antibody B

HINT

Blood groups often cause confusion but it will help if you remember that the antibodies present in the plasma cannot be the same as the antigens on the red blood cells. For example, a person with AB has both antigens, so therefore cannot have either antibody A or antibody B while someone with group O will have both.

This will be marked on a "sliding scale" with all 6 correct needed to obtain the 2 marks. 4 or 5 correct will obtain 1 mark and anything less will receive no marks.

(*b*) AB, A, B and O. [1] PS

HINT

Remember when solving this kind of question that the donor's red blood cells must be compatible with the recipient's blood plasma in which antibodies may be present. Someone who is blood group AB has neither antibody A nor antibody B present so can receive blood from anyone. Such a person is called a universal recipient.

(*c*) Blood group O can be given to any of the four blood groups. [1] KU

(*d*) (i) Water concentration on either side of the membrane is the same.

No net movement of water takes place between the plasma and the contents of the red blood cell.

[2] KU

HINT

Here we have an osmotic balance set up between the blood plasma and the internal contents of the red blood cells so that there is no water concentration gradient. Notice that two points are needed here.

(ii) Red blood cells are biconcave.

and

This presents a very large surface area for exchange of materials. [1] KU

HINT

Both points are needed here.

3. (*a*) [2] PS

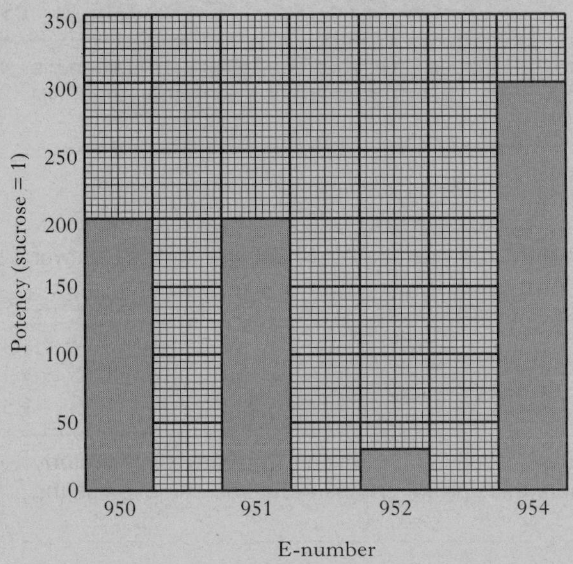

> *HINT*
>
> Remember, when constructing bar charts, always label each axis correctly and include units where appropriate. Also, separate each bar by the same spacing, make each bar the same width, use more than 50% of the grid and draw each bar with a ruler very carefully. Notice the use of bold type to draw your attention to a particular instruction, here to draw a bar chart and not, for example, a line graph.
>
> One mark for labelling each axis correctly and one mark for correct plotting of the data.

(*b*) 7 × 65 = 455 mg. [1] PS

(*c*) Reduce the intake of the sweetener/children are more susceptible to the effects of sweeteners than adults. [1] PS

4. (*a*) Stage 1: Glycolysis

Stage 2: Krebs cycle

Stage 3: Electron transport chain/hydrogen carrier system/cytochrome system [2] KU

> *HINT*
>
> Students often find the reactions of aerobic respiration difficult but this lends itself very well to a diagrammatic representation. You need to know all the intermediates, the number of carbon atoms in each, where carbon dioxide comes off and where hydrogen comes off.
>
> All three correct answers for both marks. Two correct for one mark.

(*b*) Mitochondrion [1] KU

> *HINT*
>
> Another example where a fully-labelled diagram, showing not just the structures of the organelle but also the functions, would be of great benefit.

(*c*) Acetyl group (via acetyl Co A)

Hydrogen. [2] KU

(*d*) ATP/adenosine triphosphate [1] KU

(*e*) Glucose [1] KU

5. (*a*) Huntington's disease [1] PS

The condition appears in each generation.

Each affected person has an affected parent.

If both parents are unaffected, the condition does not appear in the next generation. [2] PS

> *HINT*
>
> Notice that males and females are affected by this disease so it is not sex-linked. Also, the disease is expressed in relatively high numbers which means it is unlikely to be recessive. This leads, by elimination, if you were not able to work it out from first principles, to the conclusion that the disease is autosomal dominant and therefore Huntington's.

5. (Continued)

(*b*) 50% [1] PS

> **HINT** If you represent the allele for Huntington's disease by H, then A's father is Hh (since his daughter is unaffected) and his mother is hh. Therefore, there is a 50% chance he will inherit the allele causing the disease.

(*c*) 250 [1] PS

> **HINT** Half of 5,000,000 is 2,500,000 and when you divide this by 10,000 you get the answer of 250.

(*d*) Chorionic villus sampling [1] KU

6. (*a*) 4·5 months/18 weeks [1] PS

> **HINT** Remember that human pregnancy lasts (usually) 9 months and you are told the study was on the second half so that is where this answer comes from. You can express the answer in months or weeks.

(*b*) 1150 [1] PS

> **HINT** Here you have to add up each number of births as follows, starting at the top of graph 1: 380+140+100+340+100+90.

(*c*) 20·8% [1] PS

> **HINT** In total there were 140+100 women. To obtain the percentage, you have to carry out the following calculation: (240÷1150) x 100.

(*d*) Birth mass [1] PS

> **HINT** There is no need to do the actual % calculations to work out the decrease since it is obvious from the data the birth mass decreases most.

(*e*) More babies are born overall.
Birth mass is greater.
The circumference of the head is greater.
The length of the baby is greater. [2] PS

> **HINT** Any two of these for two marks.

(*f*) Use a larger sample/continue the study over a period of years/measure other features of new-born babies (such as brain function). [1] PS

> **HINT** Asking about increasing reliability in experimental results is a common question in the National Examinations!

(*g*) Improve health education/target pregnant women/advertise in antenatal clinics/involve family doctors in raising awareness. [1] PS

7. (*a*) X umbilical cord Y cervix [1] KU

(*b*) Supplies fetus with oxygen/maternal antibodies/glucose/removes carbon dioxide/fetal wastes/urea. [2] KU

> **HINT** Any two of these for both marks.

(*c*) Pathogens/viruses/thalidomide/alcohol/heroin/nicotine/carbon monoxide [1] KU

> **HINT** There are a number of potentially harmful agents which could damage a developing fetus. Only one is required here.

7. (Continued)

(*d*) Oestrogen [1] KU

HINT: The watery mucus coincides with high levels of oestrogen which comes just before ovulation. In this way, the sperm can pass through the cervix more easily.

8. (*a*) Instead of learning by rote, if we form a mental image which sounds like the word we are trying to learn, we can remember more. [1] PS

HINT: You may not use these precise words but if your answer captures the general meaning, you will get the mark.

(*b*) Increasing the size of the sample/repeating the experiment many times/use different languages.

[1] PS

HINT: Again, there are several ways of answering this but you should be aware that the psychologists who carried out this research did not limit themselves to just this scenario!

(*c*) Allow subjects to make up their own images and keywords. [1] PS

HINT: In fact, the psychologists did just this, allowing subjects to make up their own images and keywords, but they found this was also much less effective that the experimental set-up of giving the subjects the images and keywords.

(*d*) The method will not work if the foreign word does not have a direct translation in English.

[1] PS

HINT: This is quite a difficult concept to grasp. Only if the foreign word can be translated directly into a word in English will this strategy work as illustrated here.

9. (*a*) Multiple (alleles) [1] KU

(*b*) [2] KU

Blood group	*Genotype(s)*
A	AO, AA
AB	AB
O	O

HINT: It is easy to get confused between the blood group phenotypes (actual groups, A, B, AB and O) and the blood group genotypes (AA, AO, BB, BO, AB and OO). Practice working with questions on this topic.

Three correct rows will obtain two marks and any two correct rows will obtain one mark. One correct row will not obtain any marks here.

(*c*) A and B [1] PS

HINT: The man is genetically AB and the woman OO. This gives AO (group A) and BO (group B) for the possible genotypes of their children.

(*d*) Sticking/clumping together of red blood cells. [1] KU

(*e*) Advantage: Reduce the body's immune response to the transplant/inhibit the production of antibodies against the transplant.

Disadvantage: The patient is more liable to pick up infections/be unable to fight off disease.

[2] KU

10. (*a*) Pancreas [1] KU

Insulin [1] KU

10. (Continued)

(*b*) (i) Glycogen [1] KU
(ii) It is insoluble [1] KU

HINT — Since blood is mostly water, it is important that the storage form of glucose, glycogen, is insoluble. If it were not, it would be washed away by the blood flowing through the liver and muscles.

(*c*) Process brings blood sugar back to normal when it goes above or below a set point.
Once change has been been made, the correcting mechanism is switched off. [2] KU

HINT — Notice two points are required here for both marks. Feedback mechanisms operate all over the body and most are negative as shown here. They are needed to keep the body's variables, such as temperature, blood sugar levels, heart rate and breathing rate, within narrow limits. A concept known as homeostasis.

(*d*) Adrenaline [1] KU

11. (*a*) Imitation [1] KU
(*b*) Learning to use a machine/perform new task/perform sport. [1] KU

HINT — There are a variety of possible answers here but the main thing is to show that humans can learn by imitation in adult tasks by watching people who are technically accomplished in those tasks and then trying to copy them.

(*c*) Positive: Verbal praising/giving a sweet/smiling when task is performed correctly. [1] KU

HINT — There are many examples of positive reinforcement. Three are given here as ways to enhance positively someone's learning.

Negative: Shouting/angry expression on face/disapproving tone of voice. [1] KU

HINT — Similarly, there are many examples of negative reinforcement. Three are given here as ways to modify someone's behaviour by using a negative strategy of reinforcement.

(*d*) Maturation
Inheritance
Environment [2] KU

HINT — All three answers are needed for two marks. Two or one correct would obtain one mark.

Orderly sequence of stages in development.
Genes can determine how behaviour develops.
How a child is reared/type of surroundings child is exposed to. [1] KU

HINT — There are other possible explanations here but basically, you should be aiming to try and capture the sense of those given here.

12. (*a*) Autonomic, medulla, increase [1] KU
(*b*) Speeds up the rate of transmission of a nerve impulse. [1] KU

HINT — Notice this is quite a full answer here and you should aim to give all the information.

(*c*) Antagonistic/antagonism [1] KU

HINT — You have met this term before, for example, in the actions of the biceps and triceps muscles which have opposite actions to each other.

12. (Continued)

(*d*) [2] KU

Part	*Description*
Axon	Carries information toward the central nervous system
Dendron	Carries information away from the central nervous system/carries information towards the cell body
Cell body	Where the cell nucleus is located

HINT All three answers are needed for both marks. Two correct would obtain one mark.

13. (*a*) [1] PS

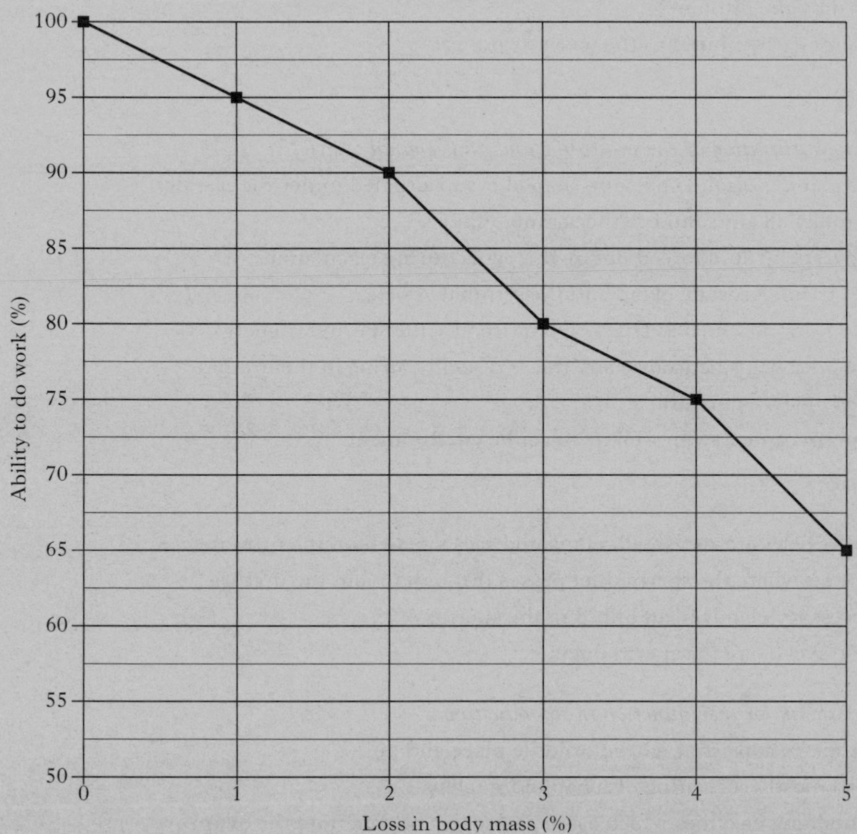

HINT Notice the *y*-axis on this graph does not begin with a zero value. Most of the graphs you are presented with, or have to draw, will normally have a zero start but be aware that this is not always the case. Make sure you label the *x*-axis carefully and include the %.

(*b*) No

The actual data do not show an exact decrease of 10% for every 1% loss in body mass. [1] PS

(*c*) Sample size may have been too small/no females in sample/no indication of ages/type of work may not have been the same for each subject. [1] PS

HINT There are other possible answers here and if you give a valid alternative, you will obtain the credit.

(*d*) 75% of 70 kg = 52·5 kg water

Decrease in ability to do work of 10% is due to loss of 1% of water.

1% of 52·5 kg = 0·525 kg [2] PS

HINT If you obtained a wrong answer for the mass of water but used the correct method of calculating the mass of water lost, you would not lose two marks here, only one. However, if you study the working, you can see how the figures have been obtained.

SECTION C

1. A (i) *Structure and function of the testes*

- Organs suspended in the scrotum
- Produce male gametes/sperm
- In the long, coiled seminiferous tubules
- Hundreds of which are present in each testis
- Sperm stored until used

Any 2 of these

- Also produce testosterone
- In the interstitial cells between the seminiferous tubules
- Under the influence of interstitial cell-stimulating hormone
- Produced by the pituitary
- Testosterone contributes to the onset of puberty

Any 2 of these

(ii) *Contribution to fertilisation of the prostate gland and seminal vesicles*

- Prostate gland is a solid chestnut-shaped organ situated under the bladder
- Adds a milky alkaline fluid to the seminal fluid
- A creamy, sticky fluid forced out of the penis during ejaculation
- Secreted by the prostate gland and the seminal vesicles
- Contains nutrients such as fructose required by the sperm for energy
- Alkaline fluid helps neutralise any traces of acidic urine in the urethra
- And the female vaginal tract
- Since sperm cannot swim well in an acidic environment

Any 2 of these

- Seminal vesicles are two small, elongated sacs situated on the prostate gland
- At the point where the sperm duct passes through to join the urethra
- First accessory glands to add fluid to the sperms
- As they travel along the sperm ducts

(iii) *Adaptation of sperm for their function in reproduction*

- Human sperm consist of a head, middle piece and tail
- The head mostly consisting of a haploid nucleus
- And containing enzymes which assist the sperm to penetrate the ovum
- The middle piece contains many mitochondria
- Needed to generate energy from respiration
- To power the movement required to reach the ovum

Any 2 of these

1. B (i) *Encoding*

- Sensory information entering the central nervous system is converted into an appropriate form for storage in memory
- Encoding involves a selective focusing on sensory information
- To the exclusion of other stimuli
- A process called attending
- Lack of which leads to difficulties in remembering
- Encoding can take various forms such as a representation of the sound/acoustic encoding
- Or a representation of the sight/visual encoding
- Or a representation of the meaning/semantic encoding
- Acoustic encoding is particularly dominant in short-term memory
- Semantic encoding is dominant in long-term memory
- Especially in encoding verbal items

Any 5 of these

1. B (continued)

(ii) *Storage*

- Storage of information in short-term memory is extremely limited
- Of the order of five to nine items
- A phenomenon known as memory span
- But can be affected by information stored in long-term memory
- To reorganise items in short-term memory
- Into distinct units, called chunks
- Allows the short-term memory potential to be increased
- Information in short-term memory has only a limited life/decays rapidly
- As it gives way to new information coming in
- Information in short-term memory may be transferred into long-term memory
- By rehearsing, organising or elaborating the meaning of the item(s)

Any 5 of these

2. A *The role of enzymes as catalysts in biochemical pathways*

- Catalysts serve to increase unfavourable reaction rates
- Are essential in living systems
- Catalysts are effective in small amounts/unchanged by the reaction
- Enzymes as catalysts have further properties such as being very specific
- Both in the nature of the reactions being catalysed and the structure of the substrate
- Denatured by extremes of pH and/or high temperatures
- Specificity is shown by the lock-and-key mechanism of enzyme action
- The substrate fitting the active site on the surface of an enzyme to form enzyme-substrate complex
- The enzyme-substrate complex breaks up to form the enzyme and products
- The enzyme is now free to perform further catalysis
- Enzymes determine the order of chemical reactions within the cell
- Also ensuring reactions take place in the correct locations and compartments
- Thus essential respiratory pathways such as the Krebs cycle
- Take place in the mitochondrial matrix
- While the electron transport chain
- Takes place on the inner mitochondrial membrane
- Enzymes work in sequence
- The product of one enzyme-controlled reaction
- Serving as a substrate for the next
- In order for all metabolic processes to operate together
- For maximum efficiency of the body
- Enzyme action must be under the influence of external factors
- Such as temperature or pH

HINT This is quite a difficult question which requires you to take a general view of the role of enzymes rather than giving a list of specific examples of enzyme action which will not get the marks. Of course you can give a few examples to illustrate, as shown here, but do not go beyond this.

8 of the 10 marks available for this question are for knowledge and understanding. You should write in properly constructed paragraphs. The remaining 2 marks are for coherence and relevance.

Coherence means:

1. using sub-headings and paragraphs as indicated;
2. making sure you keep relevant material groups together within paragraphs;
3. ensuring there is a logical progression.

Any two of these gets the coherence mark. **One or less** fails to get the coherence mark.

If you include **two or more** pieces of information which do not relate to the question, you will not get the mark for relevance.

2. B *Cause of blood pressure in vessels*

- Blood pressure is the force exerted by circulating blood on the walls of the containing vessels
- Caused by a combination of the force exerted by the contraction of the heart
- And the resistance offered by the vessels as the blood passes through

Maximum of 2 marks for this section.

Changes in blood pressure

- As blood flows through arteries, arterioles and capillaries, the pressure falls
- Due to the frictional resistance in the vessels
- Which is relatively low in the large and medium sized arteries
- But relatively high in the narrow arterioles
- Pressure decreases in the capillaries which
- Although they are narrower than arterioles
- Are present in much larger numbers than arterioles
- And therefore have a greater total cross-sectional area
- Changes in the diameter of vessels
- Due to vasoconstriction or vasodilation
- Will also affect arterial blood pressure
- Vasoconstriction of arterioles
- Causes an increase in frictional resistance
- And a corresponding increase in arterial blood pressure
- Vasodilation of arterioles causes the opposite effect

Maximum of 6 marks for this section.

8 of the 10 marks available for this question are for knowledge and understanding. You should write in properly constructed sections with appropriate headings, usually lifted from the actual question itself. The remaining 2 marks are for coherence and relevance.

Coherence means:

1. using sub-headings and paragraphs as indicated;
2. making sure you keep relevant material groups together within paragraphs;
3. ensuring there is a logical progression.

Any two of these gets the coherence mark. **One or less** fails to get the coherence mark.

If you include **two or more** pieces of information which do not relate to the question, you will not get the mark for relevance.

Answers to Practice Exam 3

SECTION A

1. A KU

HINT: Glucose is the normal substrate for aerobic respiration and is broken down to pyruvic acid in the cytoplasm. Pyruvic acid is then converted to acetyl co-enzyme A in the matrix of the mitochondria. All the other chemicals mentioned would be present inside the mitochondria.

2. B KU

3. C KU

HINT: You need to know the different types of mutations which can alter the sequence of genes on a chromosome. Here, in the first mutation, the gene C has been deleted (i.e. lost) while in the second mutation genes D and E have been inverted (i.e. switched around).

4. A KU

HINT: This is a slightly tricky question needing you to think through the sequence of DNA to mRNA to tRNA. The DNA base triplet ACA will code to UGU on the mRNA (remember uracil replaces thymine) which is turn codes to ACA on the tRNA. In fact, if you notice you didn't need to go through the mRNA sequence since you are back to the original DNA triplet. However, it's important you are careful with this type of question because uracil is replacing thymine.

5. C PS

HINT: First, work out the mass of urea in 1 L of blood as 1/60 x 6 = 0·1 g. 100 cm^3 is 1/10 of a litre so the final calculation is 1/10 x 0·1 = 0·01 g.

6. B KU

HINT: Vitamins are usually carried in dissolved form in the plasma or, if they are fat-soluble (such as vitamins A, D, E and K), they are carried in fat micelles into the lymphatic system.

7. B KU

HINT: This is a difficult question because it needs you to know the meaning, of all the terms used. Don't be put off by the example of amylase being used. It's an enzyme, remember, so it's a protein and therefore produced in the same way as all the other proteins!

8. D KU

HINT: Remember that meiosis halves the number of chromosomes in a body cell from 46 to 23 in a gamete which means the quantity of DNA must also be halved.

9. B PS

HINT: This is a "higher order" type problem solving question. As blood travels round the body, it encounters areas of high oxygen tension in the lungs and low oxygen tension in the tissues. For any pigment to be effective, it must be able to pick up and carry oxygen from the high tension areas to the low tension areas and offload it there quickly where and when it is needed. Let's look at each answer in turn:

A Both pigments are capable of being 100% saturated with oxygen.

B At low oxygen tensions, in the tissues, X is very much less saturated than Y. Look at the value of 10 mmHg for each. Y is now only about 10% saturated having offloaded some 90% of its oxygen while X is still about 50% saturated, having offloaded only 50% of its oxygen. X is therefore much better at releasing its oxygen where it is needed.

C At high oxygen tensions, both X and Y are equally 100% saturated.

D In the lungs, where the oxygen tension is very high, both X and Y are very saturated but X in fact is still 100% saturated as Y starts to offload some of its oxygen.

10. A KU

HINT

While the placenta does eventually produce progesterone, in the early months it is the *corpus luteum* which serves this function.

11. D KU

HINT

If the egg is not fertilised it cannot produced HCG.

12. A PS

HINT

You need to calculate the surface areas and volumes of structures (b) and (c) separately.

(*b*) has twice the side length of (a) so its surface is $2^2 \times 6 = 24$ and its volume is $2^3 = 8$ giving a SA/V ratio of 24/8 or 3:1

(*c*) has three times the side length of (a) so its surface is $2^3 \times 6 = 54$ and its volume is $3^3 = 27$ giving a SA/V ratio of 54/27 or 2:1

13. D PS

HINT

This is a familiar situation when a limiting factor is in excess. Here at point X, there is no shortage of substrate therefore something else is stopping the reaction going any faster. All the active sites of the enzyme have been used up at this point.

14. B KU

15. D KU

HINT

Antidiuretic hormone is concerned with blood water content, not with blood glucose levels.

Oestrogen is a female sex hormone, again not involved in blood glucose levels.

Insulin is involved in blood glucose levels but its presence would lower these, not increase them.

16. D PS

HINT

To get from a 10% solution to a 1% solution of vitamin requires a 1/10 dilution. This would be achieved by mixing 90 cm^3 water with 10 cm^3 10% vitamin C solution. A rather tricky question here.

17. C KU

HINT

You have to look at when the percentage growth starts and continues to rise which occurs at 10 years approximately.

18. D PS

HINT

You need to be careful not to go beyond what is given here. The fact that drug 2 dissolves fastest does not allow you to conclude it will be the most effective at treating pain.

Drug 6 actually takes longer than drug 5 to dissolve.

There is no data to support or refute how well these drugs dissolve in water.

Drug 2 takes the least time to dissolve.

19. B PS

HINT

From the diagram, you can see that people aged 85 or older are predominantly female.

Over 300,000 males are in the range 45–49 years, the largest of any of the given ranges. This is therefore a valid conclusion.

There are far more females older than 20 years in this sample.

In the oldest range, there are fewer males than females.

20. D KU

HINT The aorta is the largest artery in the body receiving blood under very high pressure from the contraction of the left ventricle.

21. D KU

HINT Because both parents are normal, each must have at least one dominant form of the gene but since they have an albino child, who must be aa, each parent must also be carrying a recessive form of the gene.

22. D KU

HINT There are a number of physiological variables which can be changed in response to changing body temperature. Only three are used here but be aware of others such as shivering and changing metabolic rate.

23. B KU

HINT Lowering the yield per unit area is not beneficial, even though increasing nutritional content is.

24. A PS

HINT The simplest way to do this question is to take a ruler and carefully extend the line to 9 minutes where it cuts the *y*-axis at 80 beats per minute.

25. B PS

HINT In order to make a secondary response, the person must first of all have been exposed to the antigen and all three persons were so exposed.

26. C KU

27. D KU

HINT Social facilitation is increased performance, often with others watching as in competitions.

Deindividuation is loss of one's personal identity within a group.

Internalisation occurs when one's belief systems are changed as a result of persuasion.

Peer, sometimes called group, pressure occurs when enough people put pressure on an individual to make him or her change their mind about something.

28. A KU

29. D KU

30. D KU

SECTION B

1. (*a*) Golgi apparatus/body/complex

Processing proteins/fats/making proteins/fats ready for secretion [2] KU

(*b*) Salivary glands secrete amylase which is a protein [1] KU

> HINT: Remember that enzymes, such as amylase, are made up of protein molecules.

(*c*) Contain powerful digestive enzymes which can break down worn out or damaged cells/cell structures. [1] KU

(*d*) Phagocyte/monocyte/macrophage [1] KU

> HINT: Phagocytosis involves the engulfing and destruction of foreign agents. The process requires the bursting of the lysosomes to release the powerful and destructive enzymes to carry out the destruction.

(*e*) Pinocytosis/endocytosis [1] KU

2. (*a*) 3 hours [1] PS

> HINT: After 2.5 hours, the concentration in the mucus with the drug is 2 $\mu g/cm^3$ compared with no drug at 0·5 $\mu g/cm^3$. This is a difference of four times in the presence of the drug.

(*b*) With the drug, the concentrations in all the mucus samples are always higher than without the drug.

With the drug, concentration in the mucus samples reaches much higher level than without the drug.

With the drug, after 1 hour, the concentration in the mucus sample is much higher than without the drug.

With the drug, the concentration in the mucus samples stays at a higher level than without the drug.

[2] PS

> HINT: There are several other differences which could be given but notice the precise use of the language in answering. It is possible to state the same differences in reverse by starting with "Without the drug…"
>
> Any two valid differences, such as are given here, would each get one mark.

(*c*) Sample size was very small

No indication of gender

No indication of level of infection

One group is given an additional drug but the control group was not given a mock/placebo type drug [2] PS

> HINT: Again, there are several other design features which would invalidate a proper conclusion.
>
> Any two valid features, such as are given here, would each get one mark.

(*d*) The use of the additional drug raises the level of antibiotic in the mucus samples. [1] PS

> HINT: As before, it is acceptable to turn this round and say "Without the use of the drug…"

3. (*a*) Competitive

Inhibitor and substrate are very similarly shaped/inhibitor attaches to the active site. [2] KU

> HINT: Non-competitive inhibitors do not normally attach to the active site but instead become attached to another part of the molecule. Here, it is clear the inhibitor is attaching to the active site.

3. (continued)

(*b*) The ability of the inhibitor to slow down the reaction would decrease.

As concentration of substrate increases, more of the active sites are likely to be occupied by the substrate rather than by the inhibitor. [2] KU

(*c*) Cytochrome oxidase [1] KU

4. (*a*) P2 [1] PS

This person has four bands which overlap with the sample from the scene whereas the others have only three or two. [1] PS

(*b*) Because half of a person's genes comes from the mother and half from the father. [1] KU

(*c*) In paternity cases/deciding who the real parents of a child are/possible contamination of food. [1] KU

(*d*) Father's father

The Y chromosome can only be inherited from the father of each of the previous generations. [2] KU

> *HINT* This is quite a tricky question which needs you to think carefully about how the Y chromosome is passed from one generation to the next from father to son, never from mother to son.

(*e*) Autosomes [1] KU

5. (*a*) (i) Pituitary gland [1] KU

(ii) X follicle stimulating hormone/FSH

Y interstitial cell stimulating hormone/ICSH [1] KU

(iii) Exerts negative feedback on the pituitary/causes pituitary to secrete less FSH and less ICSH. [1] KU

> *HINT* This is yet another example of a negative feedback mechanism.

(b) Low sperm count/sperm which do not function properly.

Testosterone supplements. [2] KU

(*c*) Stimulates contractions of the uterus/labour. [1] KU

6. (*a*) 1 arteriole/artery

2 lymphatic vessel/duct [1] KU

> *HINT* Strictly speaking, a tiny artery is more properly called an arteriole than an artery.

(*b*) Decrease in oxygen/increase in carbon dioxide/decrease in glucose/increase in urea/blood pressure would decrease. [2] KU

> *HINT* There are several answers possible, some of which are shown here. Any two correct will obtain the marks.

(*c*) Arrows showing fluid moving away from capillary network. [1] KU

(*d*) Lymph [1] KU

(*e*) Protein

Too large/big to pass out of the capillary. [2] KU

7. (*a*) (i) Maximum heart rate stays higher longer than fertility.

Fertility stays at 100% for longer than maximum heart rate.

Fertility falls rapidly after 25 years compared with maximum heart rate which falls at a steady, slower rate.

Fertility reaches a 0% value whereas maximum heart rate does not.

Fertility falls faster than maximum heart rate from ages 25 to 50 years. [2] PS

> *HINT* There are a variety of valid conclusions from this data.
>
> Any two of these would each get one mark.

7. (continued)

(ii) 65% [1] PS

HINT: Each ten years the maximum heart rate falls by approximately 5%. At 70 years it is 70% so at 80 years it will be 65%.

(iii) 15 and 20 years [1] PS

HINT: The fertility rises by 65%, the greatest change for any 5 year period.

(iv) 5 years [1] PS

HINT: Between the ages of 20 and 25 years.

(*b*) 4 [1] PS

HINT: 25% of 200 = 50 women aged 40 years or more. Of this 40, 8% will experience menopause. 8/100 x 50 = 4.

8. (*a*) Liver, deamination, ammonia, urea [3] KU

HINT: All four correct answers to obtain three marks. Three or two for two marks and one correct for one mark.

(*b*) (i) X small intestine/duodenum
Y bile duct
Z gall bladder [3] KU

(ii) Bile
Emulsifies fats/lubricates food [2] KU

9. (*a*) Pancreas [1] KU

(*b*) X insulin
Y glucagon [2] KU

HINT: Remember these hormones are antagonists of each other, that is, they have opposite effects. Insulin will reduced blood glucose levels by stimulating its conversion to glycogen in the liver while glucagon will have the opposite effect.

(*c*) Rise in blood glucose level is detected.
Process brings glucose levels back to normal.
Once normal levels are reached the corrective mechanism is switched off. [2] KU

HINT: Of these statements, the second and third are the most important but you should aim to include all three to obtain full marks.

(*d*) (i) Increasing levels of carbon dioxide in the blood. [1] KU

HINT: Notice, it is not enough to say carbon dioxide without reference to increasing levels.

(ii) Medulla [1] KU

HINT: Do not say "in the brain" because this is not specific enough. You are expected to know the precise location.

10. (*a*) There is no indication of whether the subjects all were originally caffeine drinkers.

The poorer performance of the people given no caffeine could have been due to the effect of not having any caffeine.

The people on the caffeine drink could simply be performing at their 'normal' levels and not necessarily showing an improvement.

It may take longer than 24 hours for caffeine to leave the body. [2] PS

> *HINT*
>
> If a person does/does not intake caffeine regularly, the effect of giving them a caffeine drink could well be very different. Ideally, all the subjects should be either regular partakers or regular abstainers.
>
> It is well known that people who take caffeine regularly and then have this withdrawn have lower performance due to poor alertness, becoming tired and so forth. The people on the non-caffeine drink could be performing badly for this reason.
>
> There is no way of knowing if the enhanced performance of the caffeine drinkers is any better or any worse that what they would normally achieve.
>
> It is known that it can take much longer than 24 hours for caffeine to leave the body completely.
>
> There are other possible reasons. Any two of these given or reasonable alternatives would each obtain one mark.

(*b*) Ensure the subjects were all regular caffeine drinkers/abstainers.

Do not divide the subjects into two groups but devise a method for tagging what they drink so they are unaware of being in one or other group.

Make sure the experimenters are unaware of what each drink contains. [2] PS

> *HINT*
>
> Be careful here not to duplicate what you have said in (a) above. Make sure you give alternatives changes in the experimental design which don't use the answers you have already given.
>
> It is an improvement on the design of the experiment not to allocate people into groups, even if the person doesn't know whether or not they are receiving a caffeine or non-caffeine drink. These types of experiments are always performed double-blind with both the subjects and the experimenters being unaware of what is in the drink, in this case.
>
> There are other design improvements and, so long as you don't duplicate anything, you would get one mark for each correct suggestion.

11. (*a*) Synapse/synaptic cleft [1] KU

(*b*) Axon Dendron [2] KU

> *HINT*
>
> The clue here is the arrowed lines indicating the flow of the neurotransmitter. The impulse is travelling from left to right. Impulses travel away from cell bodies in axons and towards in dendrons.

(*c*) Acetylcholine

Nerve impulse [2] KU

(*d*) Synapses ensure the direction of the impulse/make sure impulse travels in one direction.

Gives a place where inhibition/excitation can take place. [2] KU

> *HINT*
>
> Synapses, in some ways, act like valves in that they allow the impulse to travel in only one direction.
>
> At a synapse, control can be exerted either to prevent (inhibit) or allow (excite) the passage of a nerve impulse.

11. (continued)

(*e*) Production/secretion/reabsorption of neurotransmitters requires energy.

Energy is provided by aerobic respiration/ATP/requires mitochondria to carry out aerobic respiration to provide energy. [2] KU

HINT As always, make sure you note the number of marks allocated. Here you must give two distinct points to obtain both marks.

12. (*a*) [1] PS

Enzyme X						*Enzyme Y*					
Core	*pH*					*Core*	*pH*				
	4·0	*5·0*	*6·0*	*7·0*	*8·0*		*4·0*	*5·0*	*6·0*	*7·0*	*8·0*
1	15·1	21·9	29·5	28·8	30·0	*1*	30·0	29·7	24·0	22·1	16·0
2	15·5	19·8	29·0	29·9	29·8	*2*	29·9	28·9	24·8	21·9	15·9
3	14·8	19·9	28·6	29·6	29·8	*3*	29·7	29·7	23·9	22·2	15·8
4	14·9	21·9	28·8	29·5	29·9	*4*	30·0	29·7	24·1	21·6	16·1
5	15·2	20·0	28·6	29·7	30·0	*5*	29·9	30·0	23·7	21·7	15·7
Ave	15·1	20·7	28·5	29·5	29·9	*Ave*	29·9	29·6	24·1	21·9	15·9

(*b*) [3] PS

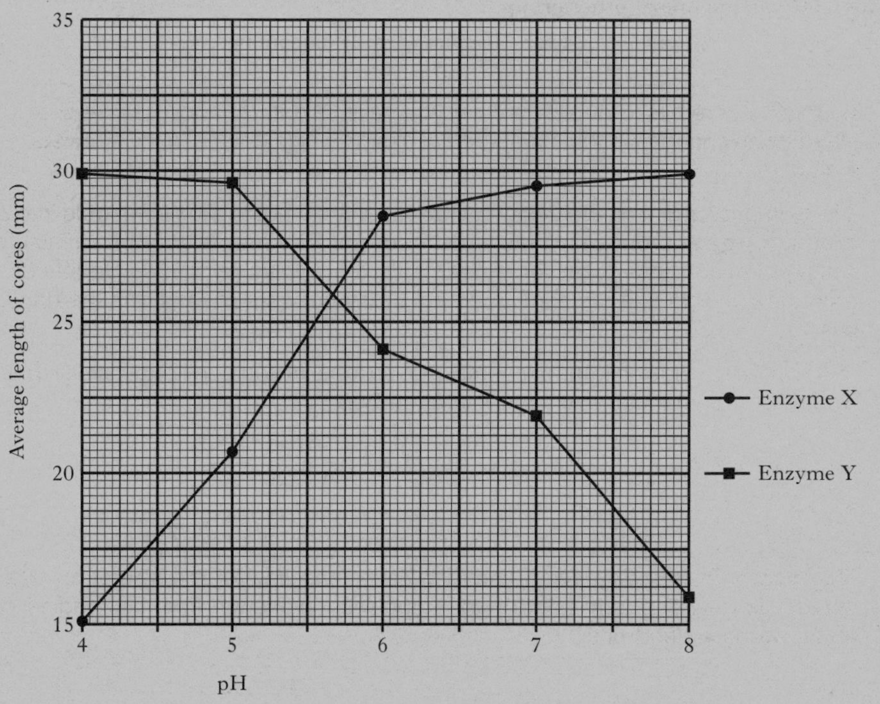

HINT Notice the axes for this graph do not start at the origin. You need to add a key at the side to distinguish each plot.

You would obtain one mark for correct completion of both axes and one for each plot (including its key).

(*c*) As the pH increases, enzyme X becomes less effective/active.

As the pH increases, enzyme Y becomes more effective/active. [2] PS

HINT Remember that the more active the enzyme, the shorter will be the core.

12. (continued)

(*d*) The cylinders were uniform all the way down/same borer used throughout/no gaps in the cores.

[1] PS

HINT

It is assumed that the diameter of each core will be the same if the same borer is used; no gaps, such as air spaces, should appear in any core.

(*e*) There was no control experiment/water could have been used instead of enzyme/enzymes could have been denatured before using.

No indication that temperature was controlled.

No indication that the concentrations of the enzymes were the same.

The range of pH values were very close/use wider range/more values. [2] PS

HINT

All biological experiments need to be controlled. There is no way of knowing if the cores would have changed lengths just by being in water alone for example. This is a very fundamental point about biological experiments.

Enzymes are sensitive to temperature so it must be controlled.

If the concentrations of the enzymes were different, this would invalidate the results.

A difference of 1 pH unit is quite a lot. It would have been better to have more discrete values, say 4·2, 4·4, 4·6 etc, and over a wider range of pH.

SECTION C

1. A (i) *Shaping*

- Gradual and deliberate modification of behaviour
- By selective reinforcement
- Of approximations which come increasingly close to a desired behavioural outcome
- Often associated with developing complex behaviours
- By combining existing simple patterns
- As, for example, in the development of a particularly sophisticated athletic skill

Any 3 of these but only 1 mark available for an example

(ii) *Reinforcement*

- Reinforcement is the enhancing of learning
- By using some stimulus
- Such as an act, information or voice expression
- Usually positive in the case of human learning
- To reward a particular behavioural outcome
- Thereby increasing the likelihood of that behaviour being repeated
- As seen, for example, in the judicious use of praise by a teacher working with young children

Any 4 of these but only 1 mark available for an example

(iii) *Extinction*

- Gradual decay of a particular learned response
- When the reinforcement of that response is withdrawn or reduced
- And may account for the fading of particular motor skills through lack of usage
- Type of reinforcement used heavily influences extinction
- Behaviour which has been learned using negative reinforcement
- Being relatively resistant to extinction
- Behaviour which has been learned using positive reinforcement
- Is much more liable to decay

Any 4 of these

Always use the lettering given, here (i), (ii) and (iii), and it is a good idea to use the actual text of the subheading as well, to help keep the material relevant to that part of the question.

1. B (i) *Relationship between structure and function*

- Red cells have no nucleus
- Or other sub-cellular organelles
- Giving cells unrestricted space to carry haemoglobin
- For maximum oxygen uptake
- Their small size/about 8 μm in diameter
- And biconcave shape
- Present a very large surface area in relation to volume
- The membrane is flexible
- Allowing the cells to squeeze through narrow capillaries unhindered

Any 4 of these

(ii) *Production and eventual breakdown*

- Red cells are produced in bone marrow
- Originate from unspecialised stem cells
- Potentially at a very high rate/2·5 million cells per second
- In order to maintain the red cell count rate of formation must balance the rate of loss
- This rate, which is subject to feedback control
- Stimulated by the oxygen levels in the blood
- When low an increase in the rate of cell production

1. B (continued)

- When high a decrease in the rate of cell production
- Thereby maintaining blood viscosity and homeostasis
- Red cells, having no nucleus, have a limited life span/120 days
- Worn out red cells may be phagocytosed in the spleen, liver and bone marrow
- The haemoglobin is broken down to haem and globin
- To be recycled in the marrow
- And the remainder being excreted by the liver
- As a bile pigment called bilirubin

Any 6 of these

2. A *Structure of the plasma membrane*

- Cells are surrounded by a selective membrane
- Complex elastic covering which separates the internal from the external environment
- Consisting of phospholipids and proteins
- The types of lipids and proteins vary across different cell types
- Structure only visible under the electron microscope
- Is known as a fluid-mosaic
- Mobile double layer of phospholipid molecules
- Each of which has a hydrophilic (water-loving) head and a hydrophobic (water-hating) tail
- Arrange themselves to form a double layer containing a mosaic of protein molecules

Notice you are asked about structure here, not function, so be careful to stick to the relevant points.

Also, this answer lends itself readily to a labelled diagram.

Maximum of 5 marks for this section.

Function of plasma membrane in active transport

- Active transport is the movement of materials across a membrane against a concentration gradient
- Requires the expenditure of energy/adenosine triphosphate
- Plasma membrane normally actively transports a particular substance either into or out of cell but not both
- Within the plasma membrane there are carrier molecules
- These react chemically with the substance being actively transported
- Carry it across the membrane
- Carrier molecule then becomes free to repeat process

Maximum of 3 marks for this section

8 of the 10 marks available for this question are for knowledge and understanding. You should write in properly constructed sections with appropriate headings, usually lifted from the actual question itself. The remaining 2 marks are for coherence and relevance.

Coherence means:

1. using sub-headings and paragraphs as indicated;
2. making sure you keep relevant material groups together within paragraphs;
3. ensuring there is a logical progression.

Any two of these gets the coherence mark. **One or less** fails to get the coherence mark.

If you include **two or more** pieces of information which do not relate to the question, you will not get the mark for relevance.

2. **B** *Aerobic*

- Needs oxygen
- Occurs in mitochondria
- Mostly cyclical pathway
- Net gain of thirty-six ATP molecules
- Major mechanism for supplying energy to cells
- Cannot function when oxygen supply is insufficient, such as during violent muscular activity – lactic acid not produced
- During exercise, rate of aerobic respiration decreases in muscle cells
- Initial substrate is a 2-carbon molecule
- Produces carbon dioxide
- Forms water
- Needs oxygen to produce ATP via cytochrome system
- Cytochrome oxidase necessary to force hydrogen and oxygen to combine to form water

Anaerobic

- Does not need oxygen
- Occurs in cytoplasm
- Mostly linear pathway
- Net gain of two ATP molecules
- Minor mechanism for supplying energy to cells
- Can function for a short time during strenuous exercise to provide energy needed – lactic acid may be produced
- During exercise, rate of anaerobic respiration increases in muscle cells
- Initial substrate is a 6-carbon molecule
- Does not produce carbon dioxide
- Forms pyruvic acid
- Can produce ATP in absence of oxygen and cytochrome system
- Cytochrome oxidase not necessary

Notice here how each statement for aerobic is exactly matched with one for anaerobic. You could indeed use a tabular presentation for this answer. Make sure you stick closely to the question which asks for differences, NOT similarities between these two processes.

8 of the 10 marks available for this question are for knowledge and understanding. You should write in properly constructed sections with appropriate headings, usually lifted from the actual question itself. The remaining 2 marks are for coherence and relevance.

Coherence means:

1. using sub-headings and paragraphs as indicated;
2. making sure you keep relevant material groups together within paragraphs;
3. ensuring there is a logical progression.

Any two of these gets the coherence mark. **One or less** fails to get the coherence mark.

If you include **two or more** pieces of information which do not relate to the question, you will not get the mark for relevance.